FILMMAKERS SERIES

edited by
ANTHONY SLIDE

In Preparation

ALDOUS HUXLEY AND FILM

by
Virginia M. Clark

Filmmakers, No. 16

The Scarecrow Press, Inc.
Metuchen, N.J., & London
1987

Frontispiece: Aldous Huxley in the desert (Llano, Calif.),
                March 1946. Photo by George Platt Lynes.
                Used by permission of Russell Lynes.

The author gratefully acknowledges permission to reprint the
following:

Excerpts from <u>Letters of Aldous Huxley</u>, edited by Grover
Smith. Copyright © 1969 by Laura Huxley. Reprinted by
permission of Harper & Row, Publishers, Inc. and Chatto &
Windus Ltd.

Excerpts from <u>Aldous Huxley: A Biography</u>, by Sybille Bedford. Copyright © 1973, 1974 by Sybille Bedford. Reprinted
by permission of Alfred A. Knopf, Inc.

copy 138

Library of Congress Cataloging-in-Publication Data

Clark, Virginia Martha.
    Aldous Huxley and film.

    (Filmmakers ; no. 16)
    Filmography: p.
    Bibliography: p.
    Includes index.
    1. Huxley, Aldous, 1894-1963--Moving-picture plays.
2. Huxley, Aldous, 1894-1963. 3. Moving-picture
plays--History and criticism. 4. Los Angeles (Calif.)
in literature. 5. Authors, English--20th century--
Biography. 6. Screen writers--United States--
Biography. 1. Title. II. Series: Filmmakers series ;
no. 16.
PR6015.U9Z5954   1987   822'.912   87-12308
ISBN 0-8108-2002-1

To my mother,

who has encouraged me all the way,

and in memory of my father

EDITOR'S FOREWORD

Aldous Huxley spent more than some time in the sun (as writer Tom Dardis refers to the years spent as Hollywood screenwriters by the literary giants of the Twentieth Century). He was a resident of Los Angeles for something like twenty-five years, and, indeed, he died in the city on the same date as President Kennedy was assassinated. While living there, he produced a number of important books, worked on several abortive film projects, experimented with psychedelic drugs (which were the inspiration for two books), and contributed screenplays to four major features, Pride and Prejudice (1940), Madame Curie (1943), Jane Eyre (1944), and A Woman's Vengeance (1947).

Unlike many of his contemporaries, Huxley was not totally reliant upon the film industry for employment, and, perhaps for this reason, his screenplays are more literate, more subdued than those of, say, William Faulkner or Nathanael West. Even A Woman's Vengeance, which is to me an unlikely Huxley screenplay, has a literate quality, as appealing as is the author's script for Pride and Prejudice.

Although it may well be argued that Huxley's screenplays do not constitute a major portion of his oeuvre, they are more than important areas for study both by film scholars and literary critics. With this volume, Virginia Clark serves both, presenting, as she does, Huxley's screen career within the context of his entire working life. She also devotes considerable space to Huxley's "Hollywood Novel," After Many a Summer Dies the Swan, and to his "lost" screenplay, Ape and Essence (which surely must have been known to Pierre Boulle when he wrote Planet of the Apes).

Virginia Martha Clark, a native of Los Angeles, holds a Ph.D. in English (including film studies) from the University of Maryland. She has been on the staffs of both the Motion Picture Division at the Library of Congress and The American Film Institute, and was involved in the preparation of the 1911-1920 and 1931-1940 volumes of the American Film Institute Catlog, Feature Films. She has also taught English and Film at the University of Maryland and at Frostburg State College in western Maryland. This is both Ms. Clark's first book and the first book in the Filmmakers Series to consider the work of a screenwriter. I am sure, in both instances, it will not be the last.

Anthony Slide

CONTENTS

ACKNOWLEDGMENTS

I am grateful for the generous cooperation of Laura
Huxley, Aldous Huxley's widow, and Matthew Huxley, his
son, in granting interviews and lending photographs. Through
meetings with them, I gained an understanding of the subject
not otherwise possible. Others whom I interviewed provided
valuable insights regarding the life and times of Aldous Huxley, and being a writer in Hollywood: Christopher Isherwood,
Millard Kaufman, Gladys and Franklin Lacey, Rouben Mamoulian, Rosalind Rajagopal, Robert Saudek and Jacob Zeitlin.

Others have given encouragement and some good leads:
Ralph DeAnna, David Dunaway, Robert Grasmere, and Michael
Van Himbergen; I would especially like to thank David Parker
at the Library of Congress Motion Picture, Broadcasting and
Recorded Sound Division. While I was writing an earlier version of this book, my professors at the University of Maryland
offered useful suggestions: Jackson Barry and John Russell
of the English Department, and Robert Kolker of the Radio-
Television-Film Department.

The staff at the following institutions have been most
helpful while I was researching the book: the Library of
Congress, Museum of Modern Art, Lincoln Center Library
for the Performing Arts, Louis B. Mayer Library at The
American Film Institute, U.C.L.A. Research Library, Academy
of Motion Picture Arts and Sciences, and M-G-M Studios.

And thanks to my editor Tony Slide for his faith and
guidance.

V. M. C.

INTRODUCTION

On the whole those who have loved the Mediterranean will not be reconciled here and those who
really care for books can never settle down to
the impermanent world of the cinema. Those
who do not love the cinema have no business to
come. There are exceptional cases of intellectual
adaptation of which Huxley's is the most remarkable. The Californian climate and food creates
giants but not genius, but Huxley has filled out
into a kind of Apollonian majesty; he radiates
both intelligence and serene goodness, and is
the best possible testimony to the simple life he
leads and the faith he believes in, the only English writer, I think, entirely to have benefited
by his transplantation and whom one feels ex-
quisitely refreshed by meeting.

--Cyril Connolly, Horizon, October 1947

When most people think of Aldous Huxley, what comes
to mind immediately is his utopian novel Brave New World.
Not generally known or appreciated is that Huxley--philosopher,
man of letters, heir to a distinguished English family of
scientists--lived the last twenty-five years of his life, beginning in 1938, in Los Angeles. What is more, in addition
to his other projects, he was actively engaged in writing for
films. How did Huxley come to live and work in Hollywood?
What were the results? These questions form the basis of
this exploration of Huxley's involvement in film as writer and
adapter, and examination of the interactions between film and
literature in Huxley's career. Through this study, placed in
a biographical/cultural context, we may enrich our understanding of Huxley, and of what happens when an extraordinary
sensibility turns to the medium of film.

When we study the life and career of Huxley, we see that it divides itself into two distinct stages, with the turning point occurring in the late 1930s. The first phase, when he spent most of his time in England, Italy and France, is marked by writing which is sharply satirical, intending to describe rather than teach. Huxley's attitudes toward film during this stage are either neutral or hostile, reflecting the prejudices of his upper-middle-class, literary-scientific heritage. He criticizes film as a mass medium, as another product of modern technology, which, misused, can induce passivity rather than creativity. The change in his attitudes and writing style begins in the late 1930s, with his becoming active in the pacifist movement and delving deeper into mysticism--preoccupations which are explored in Eyeless in Gaza (1936), his richest novel, marking a watershed in his fiction.

At the same time Huxley's philosophy had begun to change. Emphasizing a new openness and awareness, he took steps which would lead to both a new career in screenwriting and a new residency. This second stage of his life started with his touring of America in 1937 with Gerald Heard to lecture on pacifism and the "ends and means" for improving society. While there he was approached by an agent with the idea of having films made out of his novels. This idea spurred his interest in films, inspiring him to write his first scenario, Success. Remaining in California, Huxley began his film work in earnest the following year, 1938, when he worked on a treatment for Madame Curie. In the future he would receive screenwriting credit for Pride and Prejudice, Jane Eyre, and A Woman's Vengeance, as well as be involved in numerous other film projects. Huxley's writing during this latter stage of his life had shifted to satire intending to exhort, reflecting his new philosophical interests. This desire to teach by using parable is combined with Huxley's reactions to his film experiences, as well as to Los Angeles culture--itself movie-dominated--in two novels in particular: After Many a Summer Dies the Swan (1939) and Ape and Essence (1948). As we shall see, the period which Huxley spent in Los Angeles writing for films, while he continued to pursue his other interests, should be regarded--despite some frustrations--as time well spent.

CHAPTER I. BACKGROUND

First Impressions

Aldous Huxley was born in Surrey, England, at the same time that movies were beginning to come into the world: 1894. As Huxley grew up, the movies came of age. But Huxley was born into an upper-middle-class, intellectual British family with a literary-scientific heritage--a class which in general thought little of the new medium. It is this heritage which helped determine Huxley's early attitudes toward film.

As a young man Huxley went to the cinema only occasionally. An attack of blindness in 1910 at the age of sixteen had some influence in this, since it kept him isolated at home, away from school for some time (problems with poor vision would trouble him more or less for the rest of his life). One of his few references to film in these early years is found in a letter of 1916, when Huxley was at Balliol College, Oxford. He mentions seeing Jane Eyre (probably the 1915 Biograph version, made two years after D. W. Griffith had left the company), which he finds curious for its modernization and California setting: "The plot of the novel was absolutely destroyed in the process of cinematising it," he remarked, "but that is of course of no importance." He also expresses a desire to see Griffith's masterpiece of 1915, The Birth of a Nation, "which is said to be a really great film, an epic in pictures. It is said to mark quite a new epoch in cinematographic art."[1] Huxley shows here a mild interest in films, relative to his far greater and more sustained interest in literature. He could not imagine that he himself would write the screenplay for another version of Jane Eyre, almost thirty years later.

1

But there is another early letter which is far more revealing. Not only do we see the beginning of his interest
in writing drama; even more importantly, we see that Huxley
comes ever so close to recognizing the potential of film for
more and different possibilities than drama--whose conventions
he wished to reform. Writing in 1918, at a time when he was
bored with his teaching position at Eton and dreaming of
other, more exciting things (very much like Theodore Gumbril at the beginning of Huxley's 1923 novel, Antic Hay),
Huxley displays his youthful naiveté and ambition. He reports he has been writing a play, "but it is so wholly undra-
matic" and so "much more suitable for a long-drawn Henry
Jamesian short story" that he will "abandon it and reshape
it" (it eventually evolved into the long story "Happily Ever
After"). The important part of the letter concerns his comparison of the conventions of the stage with cinema--although
with his natural prejudice toward the theatre he is not fully
aware of the implications:

> Plays are obviously the things one must pay atten-
> tion to. Imprimus, they are the only literary essays
> out of which a lot of money can be made; and I am
> determined to make writing pay. Furthermore, in-
> finitely crude as they are, they have distinct possi-
> bilities in the way of liveliness. I shall try and
> write a farce.... After that, one can begin ser-
> iously considering some new and better stage con-
> vention by which some of the crudities of the the-
> atre can be overcome.... [Such as presenting
> character]. Then one must certainly get rid of a
> great deal of the realism with regard to time and
> place. Then one must be permitted to have hundreds
> of scenes like Shakespeare--the cinema has already
> given a very good example in that respect. [2]

In these ideas about improving drama's "crudities," Huxley in a rough manner was hitting upon the very ways in
which cinema differs from--or even improves upon--stage
plays; but he lacked the conceptual vocabulary for making
such distinctions. He alludes to cinema's greater narrative
capability: the subtleties in cinematic acting made possible
by the camera, especially the close-up (the stage actor acts
with his voice, the film actor with his face); the capacity of
film to manipulate temporal and spatial relationships, integrated
with the nature of film's construction by shots, scenes, and

sequences--in a word, montage. Huxley seems to have recog-
nized that space in drama is static and directionless, while
time in literature--especially in drama--has a definite direction. As social historian Arnold Hauser later discussed, film
alters the character and function of space and time, embodying more than any other art form Henri Bergson's philosophy
regarding the spatialization and simultaneity of time:

> The most fundamental difference between the film
> and the other arts is that, in its world-picture, the
> boundaries of space and time are fluid--space has a
> quasi-temporal, time, to some extent, a spatial
> character. 3

All this is not meant to imply that Huxley's understanding at this time of the two mediums of film and drama began
to approach such a level of sophistication, only that he was
beginning to analyze their differences. He had some inkling
of film's potential, some awareness of D. W. Griffith's achievements, yet was unable to follow through on the consequences
of these at this time. Not among the ranks of the avant-garde
in form, he was not yet able to pursue his ideas about reform-
ing theatre, as others such as Andreyev, Strindberg, Piran-
dello, Brecht and Artaud were to do. His major early efforts
took the form of satiric, country-house novels.

To better understand Huxley's early attitudes toward
film, as manifested in his writing up through the 1930s, we
need to understand the environment which fostered them.
Like most members of his class, Huxley preferred the theatre
to "the pictures"--which were generally considered to be low-
brow entertainment, and in fact often shown along with music
hall programs. As British film historian Rachel Low has described the early days of cinema,

> Far from valuing the film, the cultural and academic
> elite was either hostile or indifferent to it and, be-
> ing ignorant of its nature, quite unaware of its po-
> tential as an art. 4

We need only look at a few opinions regarding film during this
time in England to see what Low means. For example, the
stage director Gordon Craig in 1922 pronounced this indictment of the cinema:

> Smears all it touches. Enslaves the mind of the peo-
> ple. Rules the people as in ancient days a degen-
> erate Church ruled them. Is the brat of yellow
> journalism.

And in 1923 John Drinkwater, poet, playwright and critic,
asserted that the cinema "has no existence at all as an art."[5]

To a large extent, the lack of understanding of film as
an art form was not only a matter of class, but a question of
nationality; we must understand Huxley's origins in a country
with rather parochial views of film. The film industry in
England was fairly backward at this time, due to factors such
as the size of the country and the small audience for films,
compared with the United States; the disadvantages of the
not very sunny climate; and the traditional inflexible class
system. A strong factor was the competition from American
films, such of those of Charlie Chaplin, Mary Pickford, Douglas Fairbanks, and Rudolph Valentino, which were seen more
than those from any other country.

Reactions against the negative attitudes toward film began gradually in the mid-twenties, when some non-conforming
young intellectuals--many from Cambridge University--formed
a coterie which took a serious interest in film, especially foreign film; some began to enter film production itself. It was
during the 1920s that Huxley began to spend more time abroad,
particularly in Italy; he preferred a warmer climate, and was
preoccupied at this time with literature, trying to grow as a
writer. Had he spent more time in London, he might well
have been a part of this new interest in film as art, as was
his brother, the biologist Julian Huxley. Though Aldous was
not immediately involved in it, it is useful to understand what
was going on, and Huxley did have some connections with
members of the group.

The Film Society of London was formed in 1925, with
the purpose of showing interesting films not otherwise available to a serious, minority audience; in effect it was promot-
ing the intellectual respectability of film. Original members
of the council included Ivor Montagu--who would later make
films, as well as be the first to translate into English Vsevolod
Pudovkin's Film Technique, 1929, and Sergei Eisenstein's lectures in Film Form, 1935; along with Iris Barry--a film critic,

known for Let's Go to the Pictures, 1926, and for her pioneer-
ing work beginning in 1935 as the first director of the Film
Library at the Museum of Modern Art. Coincidentally, Iris
Barry was also once the mistress of painter, novelist and
critic Wyndham Lewis, at the same time as Lewis had begun
an affair with wealthy siren Nancy Cunard. Huxley's second
novel, Antic Hay, was inspired by the sexual rivalry of Lewis
(satirized as Casimir Lypiatt) and Huxley (as Theodore Gumbril) over Nancy (who appeared as Myra Viveash). Nancy
would turn up in later Huxley novels as Lucy Tantamount in
Point Counter Point (1928), Veronica Thwale in Time Must
Have a Stop (1944), and Babs in Island (1962).

        Founding members of the Film Society (which operated
until 1939) form an impressive list: Anthony Asquith, Roger
Fry, Augustus John, George Bernard Shaw, H. G. Wells, and
Julian Huxley among them. In fact Julian would become active
in the documentary film movement in England in the 1930s.
Outstanding among his work is the 1935 film on birds which
he narrated and directed, The Private Life of the Gannets.
Produced by Alexander Korda, the film's title capitalized on
other Korda films (The Private Life of Henry VIII, and The
Private Life of Don Juan). Interestingly, Aldous Huxley
would later work with Alexander's brother, Zoltan Korda, on
A Woman's Vengeance (1947). In 1937 Julian's film on gannets
won an Academy Award for best short subject. Another notable piece of work is his film presenting a survey of evolu-
tion, Monkey Into Man (1938).[6] Aldous Huxley's interest in
documentary film-making would develop after Julian's, but we
may imagine that had Aldous remained in London, in closer
touch with his brother rather than roaming the world, he
may well have become active in film sooner. Writing can be
done anywhere (a fact Huxley delighted in); in film-making,
of course, one cannot be so independent.

        Another consideration in understanding the formation of
Huxley's attitudes toward film is the kinds of films that were
available for him to see. For some years, both in England
and in the provinces of Italy and France where Huxley spent
much of his time, it was not so easy to see films other than
the popular ones imported from America. In London, the Film
Society presented a way for distinguished foreign films to be
seen, such as Murnau's Nosferatu (1922), von Stroheim's
Greed (1923), Eisenstein's Potemkin (1925), and Dreyer's The

Passion of Joan of Arc (1928).[7] But because of post-war
anti-German feeling, a ban had been imposed on importing
German films to England in 1918 (it was originally slated for
ten years, but was revoked by 1922), which meant that important films such as Wiene's The Cabinet of Dr. Caligari
(1919) and Lang's Dr. Mabuse (1922) were not seen until
years later. Also, because of censorship problems, certain
films such as Potemkin were not seen in England until 1928.
Since Huxley never discusses films like these in his writing,
it would appear that he may not have had the opportunity to
see them. If he had, their quality would probably have made
an impression, marking, as they do, important theoretical and
stylistic developments in film, such as Russian montage theory
and German Expressionism. As it was, in his criticism of film
as a mass media, it seems that Huxley must have had in mind
the slick and often silly products of Hollywood.

Huxley also seems to have taken no cognizance of another influential force besides the Film Society in raising England's consciousness about film as art: Close-Up, the first
journal in English to take film seriously. Published in Switzerland and London from 1927 to 1933, it was international in
scope; although it seldom could praise a British picture, it
took interest, for example, in the important developments in
the cinema of Germany, France, the Soviet Union, and Japan.
Edited by Kenneth MacPherson, its contributors included Ivor
Montagu, Gertrude Stein, Dorothy M. Richardson, Upton Sin-
clair, and Sergei Eisenstein. But even with this higher level
of film appreciation in England, the British film industry remained relatively undistinguished; the "B-films" (or "quota
quickies") made to supplement the limited number of foreign
films which could be shown in Britain as a result of the Quota
Act of 1927 did little to improve the situation. There were
some exceptions, of course, such as the films of the early
Hitchcock and the documentaries of the 1930s. But England
traditionally has excelled more in the literary than in the visual arts. Apropos of all this is the telling remark by François
Truffaut in his 1967 interview with Alfred Hitchcock: "Well,
to put it quite bluntly, isn't there a certain incompatibility
between the terms 'cinema' and 'Britain.'"[8] And for a while
it looked as though the same relationship was true of cinema
and Huxley.

Fear and Loathing of Mass Culture

The advances in foreign film-making, the interest shown
in England for avant-garde films, seem not to have touched
Huxley's imagination in his early career. We can perhaps understand his neutrality--or hostility--toward film as a product
of his failure to be stimulated by the best examples of the new
medium. During the 1920s and '30s, rather than approaching
film as an art, Huxley saw film primarily as another product
of technology, mass-produced and mass-oriented; as entertainment, a passive leisure-time activity which, instead of
stimulating creativity, induced mindless quiescence. Misused,
the movies were a kind of opiate of the people, all part of the
decadent world Huxley was describing (more than trying to
change) in his early fiction.

For example in Antic Hay (1923), a novel concerned with
depicting the delusion and imperfection of the modern world,
we have this comment by Theodore Gumbril's tailor, Mr. Bojanus (who is making him a pair of "pneumatic trousers" as
per Gumbril's instructions):

> "Cinemas, newspapers, magazines, gramophones, foot-
> ball matches, wireless telephones--take them or leave
> them, if you want to amuse yourself. The ordinary
> man can't leave them."[9]

The view demonstrated in this remark, that most people do
not know how to amuse themselves creatively any more, that
they are increasingly becoming involved in passive activities,
is echoed in Huxley's next novel, Those Barren Leaves (1925).
Here, the droll, detached intellectual Francis Chelifer recites
to himself a mock catechism of mindless modern life.

> Q. What is the function of newspapers, cinemas,
>   radios, motor-bikes, jazz bands, etc.?
> A. The function of these things is the prevention
>   of thought and the killing of time. They are
>   the most powerful instruments of human happi-
>   ness.[10]

That Huxley was more or less in sympathy with these
judgments by Bojanus and Chelifer on cinema and other products of modern technology is confirmed by Huxley's next work,

where he reports his experiences with that newest city of the
new world, Los Angeles the movie capital. From September
1925 to June 1926 he had toured India, Burma, Malaya, the
Pacific, and finally America, recording his reactions to these
foreign lands in Jesting Pilate: The Diary of a Journey
(1926). Huxley found America in the midst of the Jazz Age
and Prohibition--a buoyant time of movies, moola, and moxie,
flappers and hooch (words we could hardly imagine appealing
to a Huxley protagonist). The modern age--and its mindless-
ness--Huxley found epitomized nowhere better than in Los
Angeles, "The great Joy City of the West," its citizens be-
sotted with the joy of moving about rapidly, of not thinking,
and of being too rich to care. In essence he found it a cultural wasteland, with people whole-heartedly devoted to having "a Good Time."[11]

Huxley had indeed encountered Los Angeles during its
boom years. Things were fast here--movies and cars, movie
stars. It was a place whose cultural signifiers were palm
trees and swimming pools. And money. Where religion could
mean astrology or Aimee Semple McPherson's Four Square
Gospel, where community affairs meant going to the beach
at Santa Monica or having "Iowa picnics." It was a city of
stucco and neon, built on a shifting landscape, as flimsy as
a movie set; with scenery which P. G. Wodehouse would describe as "the most loathsome on earth--a cross between Coney
Island and the Riviera."[12] The place--and its main products,
movies and dreams--captured Huxley's imagination. The experience would bear literary fruit much later; at the moment
it just roused his ire about the perils of mass society. What
disturbed him were the qualities which cultural anthropologist
Hortense Powdermaker would later examine in her definitive
study of Hollywood: The Dream Factory (1951):

> Hollywood is engaged in the mass production of pre-
> fabricated daydreams. It tries to adapt the American
> dream, that all men are created equal, to the view
> that all men's dreams should be made equal. Movies
> are the first popular art to become a big business
> with mass production and mass distribution.[13]

Huxley had found this part of the American dream just as invalid as Powdermaker later described it; in Jesting Pilate he
had pronounced "The democratic hypothesis in its extreme

and most popular form ... that all men are equal and that I
am just as good as you are" to be "humbug."[14]

   The sketches of modern life in Los Angeles and elsewhere in America were presented sometimes flippantly in Jesting Pilate; a year later Huxley crystallized his thoughts on
the modern age and the benefits and potential dangers of
high technology in an article for Harper's Magazine (August
1927), "The Outlook for American Culture: Some Reflections
in a Machine Age." Huxley begins by making it clear that
in "Speculating on the American future, we are speculating
on the future of civilized man."[15] He then clarifies his position on cinema (and other modern inventions): it is not
the medium itself which he objects to, but rather the use
to which it is generally put--mass-oriented for the greatest
profit:

> The rotary press, the process block, the cinema,
> the radio, the phonograph are used not, as they
> might so easily be used, to propagate culture, but
> its opposite. All the resources of science are ap-
> plied in order that imbecility may flourish and vul-
> garity cover the whole earth. That they are rapidly
> doing so must be obvious to anyone who glances at
> a popular picture paper, looks at a popular film,
> listens to popular music on the radio or phonograph.[16]

So, in effect, Huxley, from a sociological viewpoint, was ob-
jecting to film as a misused mass art. In this article he also
discussed another difficulty inherent in "machinery"--the way
it can remove "man's incentive to amuse himself," as in the
past he had to do. "It is difficult to believe that general
artistic culture can flourish in this atmosphere of passivity,"
he cautioned.[17]

   Huxley continued with this line of thought, condemning
passivity and decadence in modern culture (rather the stance
of the proper Arnoldian), in his satiric essay "Silence Is
Golden" (in Do What You Will, 1929). The ostensible subject
is talking pictures--The Jazz Singer in particular--which he
has just experienced for the first time, in a cinema in Paris
on the Boulevard des Italiens (where, by coincidence, one of
the pioneers of narrative film, Georges Méliès, had his studio;
a fact no doubt lost on Huxley). Had Huxley had a different

kind of appreciation of cinema, he might have criticized the
sound film on artistic grounds. With the commercial success
of The Jazz Singer (really a silent film except for Jolson's
singing and some ad libbing), which received its premiere in
New York in October 1927, and in England a year later (it
took time to get the sound equipment), the days of the silent
film were numbered.

It is worth pausing for a moment to recall how the first
few years of sound film represented a setback, in some ways,
to what had been achieved in silent film. While the sound
films of such directors as Ernst Lubitsch (starting with The
Love Parade in 1929), Rouben Mamoulian (Applause, 1929) and
Lewis Milestone (All Quiet on the Western Front, 1930) skillfully overcame these temporary problems, many others did
not. There were, for example, the disadvantages of immobility
--both of the camera (which, noisy, had to be enclosed in a
sound-proof box), and of actors (because of the placement of
microphones)--which encouraged a return to the form of a
filmed stage play, from which cinema had long since broken
away. These problems, along with others such as synchron-
ization and editing, would soon be worked out with better
technology.

But meanwhile some critics were making the mistake of
equating film having legitimate pretensions to art, with silent
film. This hostility toward sound was silenced by an important joint statement by Eisenstein, Pudovkin and Alexandrov,
which was published in Close-Up in October 1928. The Rus-
sians, who had already pointed out the importance of the juxtaposition of shots in their theory of montage, now extended
the theory to include sound:

> Only utilization of sound in counterpoint relation to
> the piece of visual mounting [montage] affords new
> possibilities of developing and perfecting the mount-
> ing.... [This will lead to] the creation of a new
> orchestral counterpoint of sight-images and sound
> images.[18]

A film such as Hitchcock's Blackmail--which started out as a
silent, was modified to have sound, and in 1929 was in effect
the first British "talkie"--showed the possibilities of this concept of counterpoint. In a memorable scene at the kitchen
table there is a discussion in which the word "knife" is heard

again and again in an increasingly distorted soundtrack, reflecting the mounting tension and near-hysteria in a young
woman with a terrible secret: the night before, in self-defense
against rape, she had stabbed a man to death.

However, these kinds of considerations about the implications of the new sound medium were not the subject of Huxley's discussion of The Jazz Singer (a film certainly not in
the same league as Blackmail). Instead, he uses the occasion
of viewing the film as a basis for a satiric examination of modern degeneracy. First, he makes no apology for his "very
tardy introduction to the talkies," because he no longer as-
pires to being "up-to-date," Modern and Sophisticated, as he
once did (like the moderns he depicted so well in Crome Yellow, Antic Hay, Those Barren Leaves, and Point Counter
Point). Thus we seem to have a maturing Huxley, probably
inspired at least in part by all he had seen and experienced
on his world tour of a few years ago (he had, after all,
judged himself at the end of that journey, as he recorded in
Jesting Pilate, to be "richer by much experience and poorer
by many exploded convictions, many perished certainties").[19]
But his attitudes to film have changed little, for now in "Silence Is Golden" he goes on to find sound films--at least at
this point--just "the latest and most frightful creation-saving
device for the production of standardized amusement."[20] And,
among the other music-hall shows he viewed on that occasion,
The Jazz Singer in particular, with its high degree of senti-
mentalism (he found Jolson's singing of "My Mammy" especially
mawkish), was an example of the vulgarization of modern life.
The "Hebrew melodists" and the jazz bands he finds to be no
part of an artistic continuum, as initiated by past musicians,
artists, and writers; they are "in no kind of relationship with
any of the immemorial decencies of human life, but only with
their own inward decay," having become part of the corrup-
tion of modern life.[21] Something of a professional nay-sayer
at this point (part of the satiric pose), Huxley had not yet
reached the phase of "informed" didacticism that would mark
his later career.

First he would have to deal with his disillusionment with
the power of science to improve the world; it was just after
Do What You Will that he demonstrated the dangers of certain
trends in science and technology in Brave New World (1932),
a utopia set 600 years in the future. This work explored the
problems of degeneracy and mass media in quite another way

than he had done previously (although the ideas are prefigured in the character Scogan's remarks about controlled population in the future, set forth in Crome Yellow eleven years
earlier). In Brave New World two of the most memorable phe-
nomena are the wonder drug "soma" ("Take a holiday from
reality whenever you like, and come back without so much
as a headache or a mythology"),[22] and the "feelies," "pictures that you could hear and feel and smell, as well as
see."[23] These feelies are turned out by the "Bureau of
Propaganda by Feeling Picture"; there is also the "Feelytone
News," obviously mocking Movietone News.

In this world, to go to the feelies was to participate in
a total sensory experience. What was it like? When John and
Lenina attended, the scent organ was playing a "delightfully
refreshing Herbal Capriccio"; when the "final blast of thyme"
had died away, the synthetic music machine started up, with
a trio for "hyper-violin, super-cello and oboe-surrogate" which
accompanied a "much more than human voice."[24] In describing these pre-feature shows, Huxley was imaginatively elabor-
ating on what had existed in reality in England and elsewhere:
besides the music (piano, organ, or orchestra) which accompanied the silent films of the 1920s, in "super cinemas" there
were sometimes also musical shows preceding or interspersed
with the films. And while the organ had been in use in English cinemas by 1919, an expensive Wurlitzer cinema organ
was used after 1924, as well as the presentation of special
effects made possible with the Vitasona effects machine.[25]

But Huxley was quite original in his idea of having people "feel" what is happening in the film, by taking hold of the
metal knobs on the arms of the chairs. Thus John and Lenina
are totally stimulated by everything going on in the 3-D feature presentation, gloriously billed as "Three Weeks in a Helicopter. An All-Super-Singing, Synthetic-Talking, Coloured,
Stereoscopic Feely. With Synchronized Scent-Organ Accompan-
iment." The titillation of kissing, the thrill of lovemaking on
a bear-skin rug ("every hair of which ... could be separately
and distinctly felt"),[26] and later the pain of a bump on the
head in a helicopter accident--all were realistically felt. The
plot was very simple, concerning the escapades of a gigantic
black man and a blonde hovering in a helicopter for some time,
until rescued by others (rescued only because in that society
an extended tête-à-tête was frowned upon; undelayed promiscuity was the norm).

While Lenina, as a member of that society, finds the blatant sexuality of the feely to be perfectly natural, John (as a "savage" from a "primitive" society where promiscuity is discouraged) finds it an embarrassment. He will return home alone to find solace in his well-worn volume of Shakespeare, whereupon he will turn to Othello; the vulgarization of the Othello-Desdemona relationship in the feely is revealed as all the more lurid. I would venture to guess that in the selection of this couple in the feely, Huxley also had in mind a real-life couple whose affair was stirring up controversy both in England and America at the time Huxley was writing Brave New World. The affair was between Huxley's previously mentioned old acquaintance, the rich and strange Nancy Cunard, and the black Henry Crowder, an American playing in a jazz band in Venice when she met him in 1928. This "crossing over" in race had become very fashionable in some quarters of society. In London, as Paul Fussell observed, "Nancy Cunard's Black lover Henry Crowder was indispensable at any party aiming at style."27 Their relationship had peaked by 1931-32, with Nancy achieving more notoriety through her support of the Negro cause and her patronage of African art; always quite a non-conformist and a Circe-like figure, she served, as we have noted, more than once as the inspiration for Huxleyan femmes fatales.

But the important thing about the fantastic description of the feelies in Brave New World is Huxley's imaginative and contemptuous transmogrification of the movie-going experience as it existed. The novel thus presents a continuation of Huxley's negative views toward movies, and other products of modern technology, as passive amusements. This negative position on movies would carry over into his next novel, Eyeless in Gaza (1936)--which at the same time departed from Huxley's earlier work in significant ways.

Huxley worked on Eyeless in Gaza for four years. During that time, he was occupied with writing essays and traveling. More importantly, he was becoming active in the pacifist movement, and delving deeper into mysticism--preoccupations which would have an essential place in Eyeless in Gaza, concerned as it is with exploring liberation from the "freedom" of a decadent world, to real freedom in a spiritual sense. In depicting the life of Anthony Beavis and his conversion experience, Huxley was revealing much of himself. He was also following through on the tentative conclusion of Those Barren

Leaves, where Calamy finally rejects the way of self-indulgent intellectualism as represented by Chelifer, and rational hedonism as represented by Cardan, and withdraws into the mountains to contemplate the mystery of life and of the universe within himself. Eyeless in Gaza takes up the subject of how "to become aware" and "to learn to act on that awareness" in one's personal life as well as in society;[28] these concerns would henceforth dominate Huxley's life and writing.

Eyeless in Gaza could be considered the most important and best of Huxley's novels, not only because of the depth of characterization and the richness of the philosophical ideas, but in its formal achievements. Huxley is doing something with form which is new for him, and goes far beyond his attempts at using musical form in Point Counter Point (1928). In Eyeless in Gaza, Huxley experiments with a technique of manipulating time as a way of commenting on reality; in so doing, he is making use of cinematic form. The use of montage is established as a motif in the first few pages of the novel, where Anthony Beavis is shuffling through some old snapshots of people he has known, each one evoking memories (in Proustian fashion, as Beavis realizes); each one is like a still photograph taken from the "film" that will follow. The montage effect is created by the arrangement of the fifty-four chapters, each precisely dated as to day, month and year, ranging from 1902 to 1935, which are presented not chronologically but randomly, beginning with "August 30, 1933."

Thus we learn about characters, and events, discontinuously. We experience a peculiarly modern sense of reality, life presented as montage. Here is a trait of modernism, seen in modern painting, writing, film, where reality is perceived-- as Paul Fussell has described it--as being "disjointed, dissociated, fractured."[29] In Eyeless in Gaza Huxley, while decrying the empty pleasures of contemporary life, was employing the formal qualities of modernism--in particular, the spatialization of time, developed through juxtaposition (or montage)-- which are at the same time cinematic devices. With this work Huxley approaches the ranks of modernists whose novels can be seen as cinematic in form, such as James Joyce, Virginia Woolf, William Faulkner and John Dos Passos. Joseph Frank has commented on this phenomenon of montage in modern literature:

> Past and present are apprehended spatially, locked
> in a timeless unity that, while it may accentuate sur-
> face differences, eliminates any feeling of sequence
> by the very act of juxtaposition.[30]

The concept evokes a line from T. S. Eliot's Four Quartets:
"time present and time past are both perhaps present in time
future, and time future in time past"--an idea embodied in
the very arrangement of Eyeless in Gaza.

But while Huxley may be influenced by--or accommodat-
ing himself to--the formal qualities of cinema, he is above all
writing a novel of ideas. It follows that he would look to a
cinema of ideas, and continue his philosophical position on
film as a misused mass medium. For example, in Chapter 31
("September 6, 1933") when Anthony Beavis and Mark Staithes
are discussing modern views on death, an enemy even more
formidable "now that the consolations and hopes have been
taken away," Mark makes a remark recalling earlier Huxleyan
phrases about passivity and distraction, which get in the way
of awareness:

> "if you're a busy film-going, newspaper-reading,
> football-watching, chocolate-eating modern, then
> death is hell." [p. 281]

The idea is presented in another way in Chapter 23 ("June 1,
1934"), where a regenerated Anthony records in his diary
some observations about his evening out with Helen Amberley,
when they had walked along and noticed the fashionable young
theatre-goers "slouching like screen vamps":

> The pitiable models on which people form themselves!
> Once it was the Imitation of Christ--now of Holly-
> wood. [p. 223]

This wry comment on the power of Hollywood to influence behavior more than religion does is, ultimately, a denunciation
of the role of movies in influencing the misplacing or loss of
spiritual values in people's lives--values which Huxley is now
trying to stimulate people to restore.

So what Huxley is criticizing here and in his previous
attacks on cinema is not film as an art, but rather the psychological and sociological implications of film as a mass medium,

one whose power to educate and uplift had been under-utilized,
or misapplied. Part of the nature of the film experience,
though viewing is communal, is finally solitary, voyeuristic,
passive. To watch a film is to be mesmerized, to enter into
a state of consciousness akin to the dream state; sometimes,
as Huxley wrote in Eyeless in Gaza, it is "sitting at the picture palace passively accepting ready-made day-dreams from
Hollywood" (p. 355). But this suggests another aspect of
the film experience; film as a powerful ideological force.

Film holds the power to affect thought and behavior;
whether its message is political, dramatic, commercial, or
whatever, for most people, seeing is believing. Hence the
appeal of film to propagandists, whether the Bolsheviks after
1917, the National Socialists after 1933, or--in an extreme
form of the phenomenon--the "Two-Minute Hate" films of George
Orwell's 1984. But--and this is an important point--all film
carries an ideology, whether overtly political or not. According to Robert Kolker,

> film, of any period, by any filmmaker, speaks to us
> about specific things in specific ways. Its form and
> content, its fictional mode and the ways we accept
> it, are part of and reflect the larger social, cultural,
> psychological, and political structure that is itself
> determined by the way we perceive ourselves and
> our existence in the world. [31]

In his own way, Huxley at this stage does perceive and comment on the ideological nature of film; what concerns him is
the kind of ideology that film is transmitting, and how film's
potential could be used to affect people's thinking and behavior in more positive, enlightening ways.

The Artist Against the Collective

As Huxley's interests increasingly centered on mysticism
and pacifism, on finding ways of developing awareness and
one's best potentialities, his writing reflected those interests,
as did his approach to film. Perhaps the best summary of
the philosophy of life which Huxley would gradually come to
is given in a letter of 1942:

> Beauty, truth, goodness and happiness cannot be
> achieved (except at a price which sooner or later
> stultifies the achievement) by aiming directly at
> these ends, but only by aiming primarily at some-
> thing else. In a world that is busily engaged in
> destroying itself, because people insist on taking
> the direct approach to what seems to them good,
> the only thing to do is to go on harping on the
> necessity of that ultimate indirection, by which alone
> the desired goods can be achieved. [32]

These words are a logical extension of the position taken by
Huxley in Eyeless in Gaza; his position on film in that novel,
however, would undergo a modulation. Linked with this
changing regard for film is his move to California in 1938
and his subsequent work in the film medium, initially for financial reasons--an experience which brought home to him a
new understanding of the thrill, and frustrations, of a medium which he had previously known only from a seat in a
movie house, or from the perch of an intellectual. Also, his
work in films demanded that he enter into a collaborative ar-
rangement--the bane of writers.

His personal involvement in writing for films represented
a real turn-around from the younger Huxley's strong disincli-
nation to work in collaboration with others--whether in film
or in the theatre. We find his opinion clearly expressed in
a 1926 letter to his friend, the English poet Robert Nichols,
who had become enamored of movies and gone to Hollywood
looking for work in that industry (although with little success, except for a job as gagwriter for Douglas Fairbanks).
Swinging the satirist's cudgel, with a streak of intolerance
and anti-Semitism, Huxley held forth:

> A good subject to talk about, cinematography. But
> is it a good medium to work in? I say no, because
> you can't do it by yourself. You depend on Jews
> with money, on "art directors," on little bitches with
> curly hair and teeth, on young men who recommend
> skin foods in the advertisements, on photographers.
> Without their cooperation your ideas can't become ac-
> tual. You are at their mercy. What a disgust and
> a humiliation! It seems one worse, if possible, than
> the theatre. I shall stick to an art in which I can
> do all the work by myself, sitting alone, without

having to entrust my soul to a crowd of swindlers,
vulgarians and mountebanks. If one could make
films oneself, I'd be all for the movies. But as it
is--no. Surely Hollywood must have made you feel
the same. [33]

A very interesting letter, not only for the comment
about making films "oneself" (probably the closest approxi-
mation of that idea ever to be achieved in Hollywood was the
Wunderkind Orson Welles' Citizen Kane in 1941; an experiment
which could not be repeated). Although Huxley claims to find
the cinema and the theatre reprehensible (he would often take
on the pose of a disingenuous expostulator), we know that he
had long been interested in writing drama (only recall his
letter of 1918). In fact, just four years after Huxley's dis-
claimer to Nichols--with the experience of seeing an adaptation of Point Counter Point on the London stage in early 1930
(as This Way to Paradise, written by Campbell Dixon, produced by Leon M. Lion)--Huxley was inspired to write a play
of his own. His effort became The World of Light, a play
about spiritualism, produced by Lion in 1931; it prompted one
critic to remark that "He has in him qualities that may make
him a great dramatist; his day will come"[34] (an assessment
that would prove to be somewhat over-generous).

Huxley wrote to Nichols in 1930, in a fashion similar to
the earlier correspondence, about this experience of play-
writing,

which is quite fun. But God! what a horror to
have to depend on other people for your creation--
not to be personally responsible for the whole, but
be compelled to use instruments. And what instruments! It's like playing Bach's concerto for two vio-
lins on fiddles made out of packing-cases and string. [35]

In a letter to D. H. Lawrence on the same subject, Huxley
reflected wryly that "The only thing that deters one from
experimenting much with the theatre is the theatrical world."
However, he is still motivated to try: "I'm sure if one could
see one's own dramatic ideas well realized ... the thrill would
be enormous."[36]

Those ambivalent sentiments toward working in a collaborative medium apply even more to film, a medium in which

Huxley would spend a lot of time and energy in later years.
The problems of writers encountering the film industry are
legion--having one's work unappreciated, misunderstood, re-
written by others, or uncredited. Arnold Hauser takes another perspective on the situation of writers grappling with
the film industry:

> Their feelings revolt against the idea of the produc-
> tion of works of art being surrendered to a collec-
> tive, to a "concern," and they feel that it is a dis-
> paragement of art that an extraneous dictate, or at
> best a majority, should have the last word in deci-
> sions of the motives of which they are often unable
> to account for themselves. [37]

From Limbo to Los Angeles

During the 1920s Huxley and his wife Maria had spent
most of their time, when not traveling, in Italy; in fact it
was in that country that all of his novels of that period were
written. The years from the mid-1930s to the end of that
decade were restless ones for Huxley, as they were for the
world. Though the Huxleys occupied the house at La Gor-
guette, Sanary, on the French Riviera, from 1930 until February 1937, much of that period was spent in traveling about
until they finally came to rest in Los Angeles, where Huxley
would add a new dimension to his career by writing for films.
Thus Huxley was part of what Paul Fussell has called the
"British Literary Diaspora, the great flight of writers from
England in the 1920s and 1930s," [38] which seems to have been
one of the signals of literary modernism, since virtually no
modern writer, except perhaps Proust or Virginia Woolf, remained where he was "supposed" to. And so we find D. H.
Lawrence traveling extensively; Norman Douglas in Capri,
Naples, Florence; James Joyce in Paris; Robert Graves in
Majorca; Lawrence Durrell in Corfu; Christopher Isherwood in
Berlin and Los Angeles; W. H. Auden in New York, and so
on.

After extensive travel through the West Indies, Vene-
zuela, Guatemala, and Mexico from January to May 1933 (resulting in the travel book Beyond the Mexique Bay the following year), the Huxleys returned to Sanary to find a group of

German writers in exile. Escaping Nazi Germany, writers
such as Thomas Mann, Lion Feuchtwanger, Franz Werfel,
Bertolt Brecht and Stefan Zweig had found their way to
southern France. Why this particular locale? France, because it bordered Germany; the south, cheaper and warmer
than Paris; Sanary or nearby Bandol because a few of the
writers already had connections there. But by March 1934
the exiles had begun making their way elsewhere; so many
of these writers, along with other artists, musicians and those
who worked in the film industry, wound up in Los Angeles
that it was termed by some the "New Weimar." First the
Huxleys were part of the English and German colonies in
southern France, and later part of the same in southern
California (whose mild climate and film industry drew many
who might have otherwise chosen New York).[39]

The turning point in Huxley's life, his change from
being a citizen of Europe to a resident of California, began
in April 1937 when he and his wife sailed to the United States
on the Normandie (also on board, by coincidence, were the
Thomas Manns; Mann's diary reports their socializing with
the Huxleys, including going to the ship's cinema).[40] The
Huxleys were going to America for several reasons: Huxley
was to go on a lecture tour, talking about pacifism and "ends
and means," with Gerald Heard; the Huxleys wished to see
the country, meet with Professor J. B. Rhine at the parapsychology research center at Duke University, and see about
schooling for their son Matthew. At the beginning it was
clear that they had no idea that their visit would turn into
a residency; Maria had written to a friend in December 1936
that they would be in America about nine months or a year.[41]

In April and May of 1937 they toured the south and
southwest by car--Aldous, Maria, Matthew, and Gerald Heard.
Huxley wrote to his brother Julian about their visiting "seats
of learning, from Charlottesville (mouldy) to Black Mountain
(interesting), from Duke (a remarkable phenomenon) to Dil-
lard, the negro college at New Orleans (rather depressing)."[42]
They ended up at his old friend Frieda Lawrence's ranch (D.
H. Lawrence had died in 1930) in San Cristobal near Taos,
New Mexico, where they stayed until September. Life in
America, especially New Mexico, was quite a culture shock to
the very European Huxleys (Maria in fact was Belgian). Conditions at the ranch were relatively primitive; certainly the
landscape of mountains and desert was alien, as were the

Indian and Hispanic populace. Huxley wrote of that place
that "The country is most astonishing and beautiful--but I
don't know if one could stand it very long."[43]

He stayed busy at the ranch writing on ethics and the
need for disinterested virtue in Ends and Means (1937), which
took up the social implications of the credo of mysticism and
pacifism which he had arrived at in Eyeless in Gaza. For
example, he prescribed decentralization and self-reliance in
politics and economics, and the proper uses of science and
technology. It was matters such as these which he and Gerald Heard would be discussing on their lecture tour of America. With Ends and Means emerges a non-satirical essay style
indicating a mood-change in Huxley, a shift away from his
earlier "slamming" and toward a more amiable stance.

A fateful event occurred which led Huxley back to the
California he had satirized years before in Jesting Pilate: an
inquiry by Los Angeles bookseller and manuscript dealer
Jacob Zeitlin as to whether he could represent Huxley's work
to the film studios. Huxley wrote back on July 12 authorizing
Zeitlin to be his agent, and suggesting several of his works
as good film material, including Antic Hay, "The Gioconda
Smile," Point Counter Point, and Eyeless in Gaza. He added
that he would probably be visiting Los Angeles after the New
Year and "might perhaps make that stay an occasion for doing
work for the films, if something satisfactory could be found."[44]
After receiving this letter Zeitlin visited Huxley at the ranch
in August, urging him to go to Hollywood.

It is clear that the motivation for Huxley's interest in
the movies was financial; Maria would write in a letter from
San Cristobal that "After the New Year, if they offer Aldous
tons of money, he may work for the movies for a little while.
Otherwise we shall travel...."[45] Impatient to see California,
and Gerald Heard, who had gone there, the Huxleys packed
up the car and left the ranch, arriving in California in early
September. They rented a place at $1425\frac{1}{2}$ N. Crescent Heights
Boulevard, West Hollywood, which they kept until November.
Jacob Zeitlin took Huxley to the studios, introducing him to
various film people.

During the fall of 1937, Huxley wrote a scenario entitled
Success, which he tried to sell for months, but to no avail.
It is worth considering this scenario for a moment, for what

it reveals. For one thing, it deals with a theme ("nothing
fails like success") which Huxley would take up in a novel
less than two years later, After Many a Summer Dies the
Swan. The theme is especially clear in the nature of the
novel's character Jo Stoyte, a William Randolph Hearst-like
figure. The scenario also shows Huxley's rather naive understanding of what was marketable in Hollywood at this time.
As Peter Firchow comments on the script,

> There the focus is on the almost unlimited power of
> advertising to condition the masses and make prac-
> tically anyone into a public figure of major importance.
> That Huxley should have imagined Hollywood would
> even touch a manuscript with this kind of a subject
> (when it was clear that only fascists indulged in
> propaganda) reveals how little he knew about the
> industry when he first began working for it. [46]

On the other hand, perhaps he was ahead of his time; ten
years later Jack Conway made a film on the same subject, ad-
vertising, starring Clark Gable, Ava Gardner, Deborah Kerr,
and Sydney Greenstreet: The Hucksters.

The subject of conditioning, which Huxley had explored
so incisively in Brave New World, was an unwelcome, even
disturbing idea to Hollywood, since in a way they had a vested
interest in it themselves; to a large extent they dictated people's tastes and ideas through the mass medium of film.   The
situation has a parallel in Brave New World, for example, when
Controller Mustapha Mond rejects a scientific paper submitted
to him, not because it was not true, but because it might dis-
turb people's conditioning; it might

> make them lose their faith in happiness as the Sover-
> eign Good and take to believing, instead, that the
> goal was somewhere beyond, somewhere outside the
> present human sphere; that the purpose of life was
> not the maintenance of well-being, but some intensi-
> fication and refining of consciousness, some enlarge-
> ment of knowledge. [47]

Huxley kept hoping to sell the script, or to obtain other
work in films. He had little luck, and later in December he
would write that

> The best they could do in Hollywood was to ask me
> to adapt The Forsyte Saga for the screen; but even
> the lure of enormous lucre could not reconcile me to
> remaining closeted for months with the ghost of the
> late poor John Galsworthy. I couldn't face it![48]

Understandably, it was not only Galsworthy's writing style,
but the sheer bulk of nine volumes and a whole flock of For-
sytes which deterred Huxley. The adaptation problem was
eventually solved by others in That Forsyte Woman (1949),
which covered only the first book of the series and limited
the characters; however, in 1967 the BBC's Forsyte Saga
(26 hours' worth from the nine volumes) became a worldwide
success, establishing the televised novel as a powerful new
form.

In a few months Huxley would begin to have success
in his search for movie work. It is important to understand
what sort of life Huxley found in Los Angeles, and how he
would be induced to stay. Maria's October 1937 letter from
Hollywood provides a revealing picture--in a charming, offhanded way--of the Huxleys' impressions of Los Angeles at
that time. She describes it as being

> like a permanent International Exhibition. The build-
> ings are ravishing, fantastic and flimsy. They are
> all surrounded by green lawns and huge palmtrees
> and flowering hibiscus and to finish it off the popu-
> lation wear fancy-dress costume, or rather, in the
> hot weather, fancy-undress costume and everyone
> looks happy and cheerful. But it is also immense
> and of course we see many many people.[49]

These observations become even more interesting when we
notice that the beginning of Huxley's first novel after moving
to California, After Many a Summer Dies the Swan (1939),
where the Englishman Jeremy Pordage sees Los Angeles for
the first time, depicts a very similar reaction to the "fantastic" architecture and inhabitants. As Pordage is driven
around, he notices a young woman "doing her shopping in a
hydrangea-blue strapless bathing suit, platinum curls and a
black fur jacket"; in Beverly Hills he glimpses

> the façades of houses, all new, almost all in good
> taste--elegant and witty pastiches of Lutyens manor

houses, of little Trianons, of Monticellos; lighthearted
parodies of Le Corbusier's solemn machines-for-living-
in; fantastic adaptations of Mexican haciendas and
New England farms.[50]

Continuing along, Pordage gives a description remarkably
close to Maria Huxley's:

Enormous palm trees lined the road. In the sunlight,
masses of mesembryanthemums blazed with an intense
magenta glare. The houses succeeded one another,
like the pavilions at some endless international exhibition. Gloucestershire followed Andalusia and gave
place in turn to Touraine and Oaxaca, Dusseldorf
and Massachusetts.[51]

It was a fantastic place indeed, full of anomalies such
as these, and others--the re-creation of Venice, complete
with canals and arcades, just down the coast from Santa
Monica; Forest Lawn Memorial Park, full of replicas of famous
churches, statuary, and other objets d'art--which foreign
visitors, such as Huxley, could delight in. There were
touches of Europe here and there, but without the specter of
terror that was haunting Europe in the late 1930s--the en-
croaching madness of Hitler, the Spanish Civil War. California
was far from all that, in distance and in spirit. The dry climate (smogless then) was agreeable to the Huxleys' health.
And, as Maria wrote,

we think there are many worse countries in the
world, particularly in Europe (I cannot tell you how
oppressive the place was before we left it) and we
would not mind staying here for a while.[52]

But what about social and intellectual life? Would someone of such prodigious learning as Huxley, with his kind of
cultural background, find sustenance in the place he had
gleefully satirized many years ago as "Joy City"? Yes.
Partly because Los Angeles had grown up considerably from
the way it was in the roaring twenties. Also because at this
particular time, as we have noted, there were a great many
expatriates, mainly from England and Germany, whose presence in Los Angeles was a decided artistic and intellectual
boon. And then, of course, there was the lure of the film
industry. Los Angeles at this time was rather fertile ground.

Maria described their social life there--quite a contrast
to that strange, isolated time at Frieda Lawrence's New Mexico ranch that summer, as well as to the life they had known
in Europe:

> We have met here all the very eminent world of
> The Technical Institute of Pasadena, gone up Mount
> Wilson and looked at the sky with professor [Edwin]
> Hubble, we visited in country and prosperous
> ranches, we have met scholars on Bacon and novel-
> ists and sociologists and on the same day we have
> met Gary Cooper or Anita Loos or Charlie Chaplin
> and the whole pattern becomes fantastic and improb-
> able but makes one realize what could become of
> America if it went on a definite track. In fact we
> have seen so much, including the only Chinchilla
> farm in the World and the largest hogs, and the
> making of the Mickey mouse films and the working
> on orchids with mineral salts (because orchids are
> the cheapest flowers to work on as they can be well
> sold!) and oil drilling and hideous picture shows and
> the best and largest private collection of French Mod-
> ern pictures in the house of a nice mad-man.   In
> fact we now want to have a rest.[53]

Her remark about America and a "definite track" is rather
enigmatic--does she mean for better or worse? The comment
seems to prefigure a much later remark by Huxley that Los
Angeles had the "greatest potential of all the places" he knew;
but whether it was a potential "for horrors or fulfillment" he
could not tell.[54] At any rate, it is certain from Maria's comments that they were meeting a variety of interesting people
--movie and non-movie people--which is significant, because
knowing various kinds of people in Los Angeles, beyond those
in show business, would make for a much more sustaining,
enriching circle of friendship.

Thus Huxley escaped a likely fate: too often, intellectual writers (whether European or American) would come to
Hollywood, write for the movies, associate only with people
in that business, and soon become very bored and disillu-
sioned, finding the whole milieu artificial, vulgar, and mindless. This can be seen, for example, in these writers' comments on their Hollywood experiences: Hugh Walpole ("We are
all on a raft together in the middle of the cinema sea! ...

Nothing is real here but salaries"); J. B. Priestley ("I held
on to my drink and listened to talk about films, agents, Louis
B. Mayer, diet, astrology"); Noel Coward ("I'm not very keen
on Hollywood; I'd rather have a nice cup of cocoa really");
Anthony Powell ("the atmosphere of Hollywood [is] totally inimical to writing"); Somerset Maugham ("like having nothing
to eat but candy").[55] P. G. Wodehouse, whose waggish pen
demolished Hollywood's illusion of glamour, offered a description of his willing exile from paradise which summarizes the
negative sentiments about Hollywood:

> I got away from Hollywood at the end of the year
> because the jailer's daughter smuggled me in a file
> in a meat pie, but I was there long enough to realize
> what a terribly demoralizing place it is. The whole
> atmosphere there is one of insidious deceit and sub-
> terfuge. Nothing is what it affects to be. What
> looks like a tree is really a slab of wood backed with
> barrels. What appears on the screen as the tower-
> ing palace of Haroun-al-Raschid is actually a card-
> board model occupying four feet by three of space.
> The languorous lagoon is simply a smelly tank with
> a stagehand named Ed wading about in it in bathing
> trunks.[56]

Many of the writers who shared these sentiments about life
in Hollywood were also those with strong connections with
England or with the New York theatre world, who could not
find a corresponding life in Los Angeles. But Huxley's ties
with England were already considerably weakened.

    In Los Angeles his range of interests led him to asso-
ciate with diverse types--scientists, scholars, artists, film-
makers--as well as to use research facilities such as UCLA's
library (which now houses a collection of Huxley's manuscripts,
letters, and books; Huxley became friends with the librarian,
Lawrence Clark Powell).[57] As George Woodcock has observed
of the significance of this period in Huxley's life, in Los Angeles Huxley found a

> greater variety of the kind of people whose interests
> coincided with his own, at a time when he was turn-
> ing away from literature as art and towards that
> world of metaphysics, decentralist politics and the

marginal sciences in which his later life was mainly
lived.[58]

And so circumstances conspired not only to lead Huxley
to Los Angeles, but to keep him there--although at the time
it was not clear to Huxley that he would be staying. First
there was his lecture tour on "ends and means," which began
in November 1937 in Los Angeles and would take him across
the country. However, Gerald Heard broke his arm in Iowa
and Huxley had to continue on alone until January 1938, ending
up in Rhinebeck, New York (near friends), where Maria had
joined him for the holidays. During this lecture tour Huxley
expressed in a letter his feelings about suffering--or insuf-
ferable--humanity:

> I find myself often a bit overwhelmed by the curious
> rigidity and opacity of most human beings. There's
> something dismally fixed, stony, sclerotic about most
> of them--a lack of sensibility and awareness and
> flexibility, which is most depressing.[59]

What was to be done about it? Try to keep oneself open and
flexible; try to make oneself "into a little window through
which at least some light can be admitted."

After this tour it was uncertain where the Huxleys
were going to go next; they were in a sort of limbo in New
York. He was thinking perhaps Europe--but Europe was
changing, drifting into war; America seemed more and more
the place. Huxley was still waiting to hear whether he could
get work writing for films, or if his scenario Success would
sell. Where to go? At the end of December Maria had written
of their uncertain destination: "it may be Sanary, it may be
Mexico, it may be Hollywood."[60] Their fate hung in the balance at that point. But in time, word that his scenario might
be bought lured him back to Los Angeles, where he could
also see Gerald Heard, and be near his son Matthew, in
school in Colorado. So the Huxleys set off from New York
to cross America by car, arriving in Los Angeles on February
11, 1938, and rented a house at 1340 N. Laurel Avenue in
West Hollywood. And thus began Huxley's California residency. As Maria wrote,

> I would not like the East. The people are more like
> the English and freezing.... But here we have some

Mediterranean ease and kindness. We have some
friends. Not mere acquaintances. That is much
after such a short time. [61]

One of their best friends was to be Anita Loos. Huxley had met her years ago in New York, after he had seen
and admired her hit play, Gentlemen Prefer Blondes, and wrote
her what amounts to a fan letter (where we see the real Aldous behind the satirist's mask). The letter of May 14, 1926
from Chicago reveals:

> I have no excuse for writing to you--no excuse, ex-
> cept that I was enraptured by the book, have just
> hugely enjoyed the play, and am to be in America
> so short a time that I have no leisure to do things
> in the polite and tortuous way. My wife and I are
> to be in New York for about a fortnight from Monday
> 17th onwards, and it would be a very great pleasure
> --for us at any rate--if we could arrange a meeting
> with you during that time. Please forgive my im-
> pertinence and accept the sincere admiration which
> is its cause and justification. [62]

Not only would Anita Loos be a life-long friend of the Huxleys, but it was she ("the doyenne of Hollywood," as he would
refer to her fondly) [63] who would prove influential in helping
Huxley obtain his first work in the films. For Huxley, Los
Angeles would present a social environment sufficiently stimulating to bring forth new and lasting friendships, as well as
material for his scientific, mystical and literary interests.
Significantly, there is no other place he could have chosen
which could offer him such challenging and lucrative opportunities in screenwriting.

CHAPTER II. FILMS

The Romance of Science: "Madame Curie"

Aldous Huxley's baptism into the world of Hollywood provides a fascinating view of what happens when a man of his background and tastes encounters the mores of moviedom. Not only did he do respectable work, but he put the experience to his own use almost twenty years later in his novel and stage play, The Genius and the Goddess.

How did Huxley get his first movie assignment? His friend Anita Loos called up in May 1938 to see if he would be interested in doing the script of Madame Curie for M-G-M, with director George Cukor and producer Bernard Hyman-- and Greta Garbo. The project had been initiated at M-G-M by screenwriter Salka Viertel, who had read Eve Curie's 1937 biography of her mother, Madame Curie, and suggested the role to her friend Garbo, who was most enthusiastic about it. Viertel, who had written other Garbo films (Queen Christina in 1934 and Conquest in 1937), turned in an outline of the Curie story in early June 1938.[1]

I must pause here to comment on Salka Viertel as a pivotal figure in the intersecting worlds of Los Angeles: the German-speaking, and the English colonies; the literary-artistic circles and the movie people. Polish-born, an actress with Max Reinhardt in Berlin, Salka had emigrated to Los Angeles in 1928 with her husband, director Berthold Viertel (with whom Christopher Isherwood had worked in London on Isherwood's first film, Little Friend of 1934). Berthold is characterized as Friedrich Bergmann in Isherwood's 1945 novel about that filmmaking experience, Prater Violet. Salka began writing for films, as well as helping other emigrés find work in the industry. She soon developed a kind of salon--

Sundays at 165 Mabery Road in Santa Monica Canyon at-
tracted a diverse group of creative people throughout the war
years: Isherwood, Huxley, Anita Loos, Greta Garbo, George
Cukor, Thomas Mann, Bertolt Brecht and Arnold Schoenberg
among them. Many of these people would come to live nearby,
forming a stimulating community. Isherwood lived in the
Canyon, and later bought a house at 145 Adelaide Drive,
perched on a cliff with a magnificent view of the canyon and
the ocean, where he lived for many years. Garbo lived in
nearby Pacific Palisades on Amalfi Drive, where the Huxleys
would move in 1939, soon to be joined by Lion Feuchtwanger
and Thomas Mann as neighbors--just as they had lived near
one another in Sanary, the south of France, in 1933-34.
These were Europeans who liked to walk, as from Salka's
house and along the beach to the Santa Monica Pier, with
its merry-go-round, seafood restaurants, and a fortune teller
whom Huxley found fascinating.

All this was part of the life which Huxley would soon
be finding in Los Angeles. Meanwhile, would he like to come
in on the Madame Curie project? At first he was hesitant
about the idea, feeling inadequate to the task; but as he
thought more about the possibilities he became quite inter-
ested--the story of the discovery of radium was exciting,
especially to someone as scientifically-minded as Huxley.
While the financial reward the work would bring was certainly
an important factor, Huxley was ever the craftsman and took
the project seriously. But when they heard nothing more
about it for a few weeks Maria began to worry that Huxley
would be greatly disappointed if he did not receive the assignment, as we see in her letter:

> He wants to project the passion of scientific curiosity,
> and the nobility of such a life [Mme Curie's], the
> significance of the discovery of radium, the humility
> and courage of that woman. Aldous wants it to be
> done properly and nobly.... The great advantage
> of having Garbo is that she passionately wants to
> play that part; she admires Aldous and would do a
> bit more under his direction....[2]

While waiting to hear the decision they had moved from
1340 N. Laurel Avenue in West Hollywood, to 710 N. Linden
Drive in Beverly Hills, where they would spend the summer.
Finally, in a July 22 letter, Huxley could report that after

several months of indecision the studio seemed to have dᵥ
cided about his writing the treatment of Madame Curie. The
contact would soon be signed, unless the "film people [change]
their minds--which seem to have the characteristics of the
minds of chimpanzees, agitated and infinitely distractable"
(Huxley here lapsing into his favorite imagery to describe
stupidity or baseness: simian). He would enjoy doing the
job, if they left him "reasonably in peace."[3] Starting in
August Huxley had eight weeks to complete the job, for which
he was paid the princely--and welcome--sum of $15,000. As
usual, Maria had helped him with his work--by typing the
manuscript, and by chauffeuring him between Beverly Hills
and the M-G-M studios in Culver City--a commute which was
lengthened when the Huxleys moved back to West Hollywood
in September (this time to 1320 N. Crescent Heights Boulevard, just a block west of where they had been before).

Huxley submitted his treatment for Madame Curie. What
was the quality of this work, the first professional screenwriting experience of a man of letters who had for years vigor-
ously disparaged the film medium? Surprisingly, it was rather
good. Huxley's own analysis of it, as seen in a November 18,
1938 letter to his brother Julian, was:

> Rather an amusing job--though I shouldn't like too
> many of the kind, since this telling a story in purely
> pictorial terms doesn't allow of any of the experimen-
> tation with words in their relation to things, events
> and ideas, which is au fond my business. [4]

So one of the first things Huxley learned, in effect, was the
distinction between writing literature and writing for the visual medium of film. He found that scripts essentially consist
of dialogue and structure, and cannot handle abstractions or
generalities, or words for the sake of words. We may imagine
a writer like Huxley wishing to address a producer as Denis
had admonished Scogan in Crome Yellow, "You are too much
preoccupied with mere things and ideas and people to understand the full beauty of words." Against this, Scogan's reply
(with adjustments made for a movie mogul's vocabulary) would
still be effective: "A mental carminative.... That's what you
need."[5]

However, despite the exigencies of the new modus oper-
andi, Huxley believed he had turned in

> quite a good script in which the scientific processes
> used by the Curies and the trains of reasoning they
> pursued are rendered in pictorial terms (all within
> the space of about 5 minutes, which is about all the
> public will tolerate of this kind of thing!).[6]

While obviously Huxley was not about to throw away his career as a literary man and "go Hollywood," neither was he
one to abandon literary craftsmanship and do a shoddy job
on the script. And this important quality in Huxley--
craftsmanship--is displayed not only in his work on Madame
Curie (with extensive research, as well as the writing), but
in his subsequent film projects. It had been a trait of his
from the beginning of his writing career, from those lean
years in London starting with 1919 when he was just married
to Maria Nys and eking out a living by writing for journals--
before the success of his first novel Crome Yellow in 1921.
Whether he was turning out articles for the Athenaeum or
House and Garden (e.g., "Decorating Walls With Maps"), advertisements for Vogue, or reviews of (mostly bad) plays for
the Westminster Gazette, he took pride in everything he wrote.
I call attention to these journalistic writings not because they
have any lasting significance, but because they are evidence
of Huxley's professional attitude.

If Huxley displays craftsmanship in his film work, how
much artistry is there? Or rather, if there is artistry in a
screenplay, then how much is left after Hollywood gets hold
of it--or lets go of it? Raymond Chandler, a novelist with
screenwriting experience, gave his embittered opinion in his
1945 essay on "Writers in Hollywood": because of the Hollywood system--which gives power to the producer, and lowly
status to the writer (no matter how well paid he may be)--

> there is no such thing as an art of the screenplay,
> and there never will be as long as the system lasts,
> for it is the essence of this system that it seeks to
> exploit a talent without permitting it the right to be
> a talent.[7]

How did Huxley fare under this Hollywood system? Not
too well, although he turned in a fine enough piece of work.
I have examined Huxley's 145-page treatment of Madame Curie,
dated 8-26-38 and containing changes marked 9-22- and 9-23-
38, at M-G-M. In discussing it we should keep in mind that

Huxley was basing his work on Eve Curie's biography. Huxley's original work dated 8-26-38 began the story of Marie
Curie chronologically, with her parents and her childhood,
as the biography had begun. But his revision of 9-22-38
made an important, and much more cinematic change (in terms
of structure, visual excitement, and audience appeal): the
treatment now begins in medias res with a "Prologue: the
year 1921" (pages a to f), when Madame Curie comes to America, honored as the recipient of the two Nobel Prizes in
Physics and Chemistry. She arrives by ship in the New York
harbor, greeted by great fanfare; here Huxley enlarges upon
the biography's mere mention of the crowds waving flags and
of the crush of photographers. He has bands playing, crowds
cheering; "have you ever seen such a crowd?" His imagination and musical sense take over (on page b):

> The music swells up and drowns her words. Sim-
> ultaneously the steamer lets out a terrific blast of
> its foghorn. There is a marvelous cacophony as the
> band plays the Marseillaise in G major against the
> sustained E flat of the foghorn.

He then cuts to various locales Madame Curie visited in America, such as Philadelphia, and ends with Washington, D.C.
Now, cut to the first scene in the original manuscript, page
1, which begins with a classroom at a boys' high school in
Warsaw--the class of Professor Sklodowski, Marie's father;
he returns home to daughters Maria and Bronya.

These and later scenes pretty much follow the highlights of the biography: Marie becoming a governess to earn
money to go to university; meeting Pierre Curie in Paris, and
marrying him; practicing science with dedication, discovering
radium; Pierre--now professor at the Sorbonne--killed in a
gruesome accident when he falls beneath a passing horse and
wagon in 1906; Maria taking over his class at the Sorbonne--
the first woman to hold such a teaching post in a French university. The final scenes in the treatment have her giving
her first lecture at the Sorbonne, to applause; it then cuts
by sound to the applause and awards at the White House in
1921, where the story began--an effective juxtaposition and
climax.

What to make of all this? Huxley's enthusiasm for the
project--one he was perhaps eminently suitable for, given his

knowledge of science and medicine, and of the impact of the
discovery of radium--was evident. He seemed to understand
the drama of Marie Curie's life. More surprisingly, given his
limited film experience, he seemed to understand the visual
and cinematic demands. Yet his work was superseded at
M-G-M, rejected for being too "scientific"--because of the
"Hollywood system," the multiple, often indiscriminate rewrites
of scripts financed by the studio's fat bankroll; and also because of the peculiarities of this particular long-term film
project. Huxley himself was cognizant of the system when
he turned in his work:

> It now remains to be seen whether the studio will
> preserve anything of what I've done. They have
> followed their usual procedure and handed my treat-
> ment over to several other people to make a screen-
> play out of. By the time they are ready to shoot
> it may have been through twenty pairs of hands.
> What will be left? One shudders to think. [8]

Huxley was correct in his apprehensions. And the film wasn't
ready to shoot until 1943.

One of the people who had a hand in the film project--
assigned to him after Huxley in November 1938--was none
other than F. Scott Fitzgerald (who was taken off the script
called The Women, which he had been working on at M-G-M
with Donald Ogden Stewart). A brief look at Fitzgerald's
experience with Madame Curie provides a better understanding of the fate of Huxley's work. First, though, let us lay
to rest the error regarding a supposed collaboration between
Huxley and Fitzgerald on Madame Curie, as pictured by Aaron
Latham in his Crazy Sundays: F. Scott Fitzgerald in Hollywood (1971). In a chapter entitled "Madame Curie: Brave
New Heroine," Latham depicts the two writers working together on the project, looking at French newspaper clippings
about Marie Curie, and Fitzgerald thinking that each had
never needed anyone else to help write his novels, "so why
should they have to lean on one another like two cripples to
put together a movie about Mme Curie?"[9] I can find no evidence (in letters, biographies, etc.) that such a collaboration
ever took place. Huxley's treatment of August-September
1938, and Fitzgerald's treatment and revisions (dated November 1938, December 1938, and January 1939), are in M-G-M's
vault and are clearly distinct.

However, Fitzgerald apparently conceived of the approach to Madame Curie in a way similar to Huxley's--that of
a dramatic story of scientific devotion and discovery. But
what M-G-M wanted (what they thought the public would want)
was something else. A letter of February 23, 1940 from Fitzgerald to his agent describing his studio experience reveals
what was going on:

> Three months with Sidney Franklin on Madame Curie.
> We were bucking Bernie Hyman's preconception of the
> thing as a love story. Hyman glanced at what we
> had done and shelved the whole project. Franklin
> had been very interested up to that time.[10]

M-G-M wanted a love story and that's what they got--
eventually. While there is a script at M-G-M labeled "Compos-
ite Script: Hans Rameau, Franklin/Reisch/Langer, Aldous
Huxley" and dated 4-3-40, it was the final script by Paul Osborn and Paul Hans Rameau (dated 12-21-42 with revisions as
late as 8-5-43) that was the winner. By the time the film was
released in November 1943, it was directed by Mervyn LeRoy
(not Cukor), starred Greer Garson (not Garbo) and Walter
Pidgeon, and gave screenplay credit to Osborn and Rameau
(though traces of Huxley's scientific contributions are evident).
It was not at all untypical for a series of writers to work on
a film, and for only the last names (or whoever the producer
designated) to receive the screen credit.

Madame Curie proved to be a popular movie, ranked,
for example, by New York Times film critic Bosley Crowther
as among the ten best pictures of the year. It is interesting
that in Crowther's reconsideration on January 9, 1944, he
speculates on how it might have been had Garbo played in
it as had been planned: perhaps not with as much warmth
as Greer Garson, but with a "clearer comprehension of burning scientific zeal"--exactly the original intent of Garbo and
Huxley. And while Crowther finds the too-cheerful romance
and dedication of the Curies as played by Garson-Pidgeon a
bit cloying, he admires the "ingenious manner in which the
quest for radium is explained"--a contribution which quite
likely could be traced to Huxley. Crowther's final remark
on the film was:

> even if Mr. and Mrs. Miniver--or Pestle-Packing Mama
> and the Curie with the Fringe on Top--are the

characters designed to play it, it is still a high ac-
complishment on the screen.[11]

While Huxley's first effort at film writing yielded no
screen credit, the experience eventually did bear literary
fruit. The result was his underrated novel, The Genius and
the Goddess in 1955, and the play of the same name written
in collaboration with Beth Wendel and produced two years
later. The novel is an engaging tale, somewhat uncharac-
teristic of the later Huxley canon in being free of unassimi-
lated didacticism. Its poignancy derives from its depiction
of emotions as lived, and as recalled.

Although you won't find him saying so, it is clear that
Huxley loosely based his story on the life of Marie and Pierre
Curie which he had researched for the Madame Curie film.
In the novel, John Rivers, while babysitting his small grand-
son on Christmas Eve (Huxley was himself a grandfather by
now), narrates to a friend his relationship thirty years ago
as assistant to Henry Maartens, detached physicist qua "genius" and as paramour to Katy Maartens, his vibrant wife qua
"goddess." But wait--Marie Curie (no winsome Venus in her
photographs) as love goddess? Ah--that's the interesting
part. We find the key to this state of affairs in Anita Loos'
Kiss Hollywood Goodbye (1974), where, in a chapter entitled
(appropriately enough) "M-G-M Makes Room for a Genius," she
relates her memories of Aldous Huxley. It seems that while
Huxley was researching Madame Curie's life for the film, he
had sent away for a file of pertinent French newspaper clippings. They revealed some startling information--and not of
the sort he could use in the film:

> Spread out on Aldous's desk were a number of news-
> paper clippings on an aspect of the Curie romance
> we'd never heard about. A certain journalistic sleuth
> had uncovered a "love nest" in a shoddy Paris hotel
> where Marie Curie held trysts with her husband's
> young assistant. There was even a photograph of
> the room, bare of furniture except for a double bed.
> But over the headboard there hung a large framed
> portrait of, guess who? Pierre Curie![12]

In Eve Curie's biography of her mother, this scandal
was presented as a scurrilous attack by the press, and glossed
over in the most oblique way possible--and understandably so.

In fact, without outside knowledge of the matter the reader
would have no inkling that the issue was being so delicately
skirted. The revelation would have to wait for Robert Reid's
biography Marie Curie (1974), which fully examines the scandal. We learn that the trouble began with a jealous wife,
some letters, and investigative reporting, resulting in the
story breaking in the November 4, 1911 Le Journal with the
headline "A Story of Love. Mme Curie and Professor Lange-
vin"; other papers followed suit. [13]

In The Genius and the Goddess Huxley makes creative
use of what he had found in those newspaper clippings. He
has John Rivers imagine--in terms of headlines--what would
happen if Henry Maartens found out about the affair (he will
not): "Famous scientist shoots wife, self. Or, alternately,
Nobel Prize man held in double slaying. Or even Mother of
two dies in flaming Love Nest." Huxley even has a scene
where Rivers makes love with Katy in the family's weekend
farmhouse, "under the eyes of a three-quarter-length portrait of Henry Maartens." [14]

But there is another interesting parallel to be drawn:
between Marie Curie as her daughter depicted her in the
biography and Katy Maartens as Huxley created her. Each
woman was totally devoted to her husband and his work, and
each was worn down by the weight of her responsibilities.
Eve Curie describes this fatigue in her mother at one stage
of her life:

> in this woman of thirty-six the sheer animal life,
> worn down for too long, was claiming its rights.
> Marie needed to cease being "Mme Curie" for some
> time, to forget radium--to eat, sleep and think of
> nothing. This could not be. Every day brought
> new obligations. [15]

There is a remarkably similar passage in Huxley's novel,
which explains how Katy--returning home worn down by the
illness and death of her mother, and her husband's illness
caused by her absence--seeks comfort and renewal in the
arms of the young John Rivers (an experience of wondrous
revelation for him, a twenty-eight-year-old virgin):

> She had to re-establish her contacts with life--with
> life at its simplest, life in its most unequivocal

> manifestations, as physical companionship, as the
> experience of animal warmth, as strong sensation,
> as hunger and the satisfaction of hunger. It was
> a matter of self-preservation.16

Thus revitalized, she was empowered to restore her husband's
health.

In this passage about being in touch with one's primal
self, however, there is a kind of harking back to the premises
of Mark Rampion in Point Counter Point: it has a decidedly
Lawrencian quality. And indeed, with some investigation we
find that it was precisely D. H. Lawrence and his wife Frieda
whom Huxley had in mind here. Huxley was quite distressed
about producer Courtney Burr's changes in his play The Genius and the Goddess (thanks to the work of Alec Coppel as
"collaborator") when it opened in November 1957; and was
disturbed by the way actress Nancy Kelly was playing Katy
Maartens. He wrote her a letter about his conception of Katy
as "goddess." The character, he said, was based on Frieda
Lawrence, who had in effect raised Lawrence--gravely ill with
influenza and tuberculosis--from the dead, and kept death at
bay for a few years:

> Katy's miracle with Henry is merely a transcription
> of what I myself saw, thirty years ago.... Every-
> thing that Katy-Frieda does, she does with her whole
> heart. With a whole heart she loves and admires her
> genius and with a whole heart she quarrels with
> him....
>   Frieda ... was profoundly matter-of-fact, ... She
> did everything ... with the unhurried, easy seren-
> ity of the heroines and goddesses of the Homeric
> myths.17

And while Frieda may have had affairs--as Katy did--she was
totally devoted to Lawrence, who was organically dependent
on her, as was Henry Maartens on Katy. This is a most interesting letter in that it reveals Huxley's real opinions of
his friends the Lawrences, as well as disclosing a source of
his fiction.

However, Huxley added a tragic twist of his own to The
Genius and the Goddess. Katy, the earthy goddess who could
with such serene nonchalance defy bourgeois morality, would

be toppled from her Olympian perch. While arguing with her
daughter Ruth--a Swinburnian creature who is herself infat-
uated with John Rivers and jealous of her mother's affair,
which she has intuited--Katy has a car accident and meets
a grisly death. God(s) shall not be mocked. And genius
shall re-marry.

To suit his purposes Huxley has embellished what he
has drawn from his experience of working on the Madame
Curie film, as well as from his own experiences with those
whom he had known. And through all that we cannot fail
to notice that the dramatic story of D.H. and Frieda Lawrence
--as much, or more, than that of the Curies--was eminently
suited for a film. That was a script Huxley could really have
written. He had been their friend in Europe, and editor of
Lawrence's letters after his death in 1930; he and Maria had
spent their first summer in America in 1937 at Frieda's ranch
near Taos, New Mexico. But that was a story that would
have to wait until the 1981 film based on Harry T. Moore's
biography of Lawrence: Priest of Love.

Shall We Dance?: "Pride and Prejudice"

Enscounced at 701 S. Amalfi Drive in Pacific Palisades
since April, finished with writing his novel After Many a Summer in July, Huxley was ready to accept his next film assignment with M-G-M (again apparently obtained through Anita
Loos' influence) in August 1939: the adaptation of Jane Austen's Pride and Prejudice. With some delays caused by difficulty in getting to see producer Hunt Stromberg, Huxley was
occupied with "Pee and Pee" (as it was known at the studio)
until January 1940; in February the studio called him back
for revisions at half-pay. The money was welcome at a time
when Huxley was having trouble with his publishers about
royalties. The salary was $1500 a week, which Huxley at
first thought an indecent amount of money to accept with
good conscience while his family and friends were suffering
in war-time Europe. Until, that is, Anita Loos suggested that
he send part of it to help them. Of course! "The trouble
with Aldous," she remarked to Maria, "is that he's a genius
who just once in a while isn't very smart."[18]

Like Madame Curie, Pride and Prejudice was originally

slated to have a different cast and director than was finally
decided upon. The New York Times on August 21, 1939 had
announced Metro's plans for Norma Shearer and Robert Donat
to play the leads, with George Cukor directing. Instead,
Pride and Prejudice, released August 1940, featured Greer
Garson as Elizabeth and Laurence Olivier as Darcy, with Robert Z. Leonard directing. Good casting (although Garson
was not a favorite of Huxley's), exemplary direction, and a
well-done screenplay combined to make a successful venture,
which managed to preserve the spirit and wit of Austen's
novel and its own independent integrity as a film.

The look of the film was extravagant; it was full of
swaggering dandies and the rustle and bustle of voluminous
hooped skirts designed by Adrian--thanks to Hollywood's
showmanship instinct in deliberately setting the action about
forty years ahead of the period of the novel (actually written
in 1797 and published in 1813), a time in which the costume
featured the more restrained, classical lines of the Directoire
and Empire styles.

The nature of Huxley's work on Pride and Prejudice
was quite different from that of Madame Curie. First, this
assignment was not just to do a treatment--a narrative synop-
sis--but a screenplay, scene by scene, shot by shot. He was
brought in to work with M-G-M screenwriter Jane Murfin, who
apparently had already begun working on the scenario (her
latest screen credit, shared with Anita Loos, had been The
Women in 1939, the project from which F. Scott Fitzgerald
had earlier been removed). In a collaborative effort, it is
usually tricky to guess who was responsible for what in a
script, but we may assume that Huxley had a large part in
the literate dialogue and in the intelligent handling of Austen's
ironic wit, while Murfin's Hollywood experience was a factor
in determining the structure and pace.

Another complexity is that the film is an adaptation--of
a literary classic, no less--which always brings up questions
regarding the delicate balance between fidelity to source and
the effectiveness of the film in its own right. We might best
regard an adaptation of a literary work to the screen as a
critical interpretation of that work. In this case Huxley and
Murfin were not only working from Austen's novel, but from
the stage adaptation--a great success in New York and London
in 1935-36--by the Australian Helen Jerome (who received

screen credit for source material). While the Huxley-Murfin
scenario draws much from Austen, and some from Jerome's
narrative restructuring and dialogue, it often departs from
them as well. Thus there are really four texts here: Austen's
novel, Jerome's adaptation, Huxley-Murfin's script, and the
film itself--for the screenplay is not the movie.

Perhaps the best way to begin an analysis of Huxley's
achievement with Pride and Prejudice is to examine his own
conception of what he was doing. His letter of November 2,
1939 reveals his apprehensions about the vicissitudes involved
in translating the novel for the screen:

> I work away at the adaptation of Pride and Prejudice
> for the moment--an odd, cross-word puzzle job. One
> tries to do one's best for Jane Austen; but actually
> the very fact of transforming the book into a pic-
> ture must necessarily alter its whole quality in a
> profound way. [19]

Yet this alteration is not a bad thing, but a necessity; an
adaptation can be moving in its own way, but cannot repro-
duce the experience of reading the book. A film which slav-
ishly imitates a book can lead to disaster; as, for example,
Francis Ford Coppola's screenplay for The Great Gatsby in
1974--faithful to Fitzgerald, but a visually magnificent failure
as drama. The screenwriter-director Abraham Polonsky (Body
and Soul, Force of Evil) had a provocative comment on the
problem of adaptation, one which sheds some light on Huxley's
concerns:

> Adapting a book to film is fundamentally a moral
> crisis. Assuming the intention is serious, the book
> is not chosen to be translated for non-readers but
> because still embedded in the conception is a whole
> unrealized life whose language is a motion of images.
> Where a book is unfulfilled a frightful problem arises.
> The film, if successful, is a critique of the author's
> failures. [20]

Huxley goes on in his letter to express concern about
falsifying the ironic thrust of Austen's writing:

> In any picture or play, the story is essential and
> primary. In Jane Austen's books, it is a matter

> of secondary importance (every dramatic event in
> Pride and Prejudice is recorded in a couple of lines,
> generally in a letter) and serves merely as a recep-
> tacle for the dilute irony in which the characters
> are bathed. Any other kind of receptacle would
> have served the purpose well; and the insistence
> upon the story as opposed to the diffuse irony which
> the story is designed to contain, is a major falsifi-
> cation of Miss Austen.[21]

Maybe the studio was pushing the "story," but the "diffuse
irony" of Austen emerged in the film virtually unscathed. It
seems Huxley's fears were largely unfounded, for the novel's
dramatic irony--the contrast between appearance and reality,
deception and self-deception, expectation and fulfillment--is
realized in the film through characterization and dialogue.

   In film, as in literature, character is revealed in dialogue as well as in action, in point of view and in attitude.
But film has the added capacity to convey meaning visually,
through spatial language (such as framing, and scale of image) and through body language. Thus in Pride and Prejudice
the camera gives us close-ups of Elizabeth/Greer Garson's face
more than anyone else's, which appropriately draws more attention to her character and reveals to us through her facial
expressions her inner life, her prejudice. Darcy/Laurence
Olivier's character--his pride and dignity--is also conveyed
by his clothing, posture, and carriage. However, the studio,
perhaps fearful that audiences would not sufficiently understand the characters' "inner life," must surely have been behind the few lines of unconvincing dialogue in the film which
seem to violate the spirit of Austen's subtle character development. An example is the exchange about midway through the
film (just after the garden party at Netherfield--a situation
original with Huxley-Murfin which works beautifully), when
Elizabeth asserts to Darcy, "At this moment it's difficult to
believe that you're so proud," to which he replies, "At this
moment it's difficult to believe that you're so prejudiced."

   In fact, Austen's writing--contrary to the view taken
by Huxley in his letter--lends itself unusually well to cinematic adaptation. As George Bluestone so aptly pointed out
in Novels into Film (1957) regarding Pride and Prejudice, Austen's style, and a shooting script, have much in common:

> a lack of particularity, an absence of metaphorical
> language, an omniscient point of view, a dependency
> on dialogue to reveal character, an insistence on
> absolute clarity. [22]

Probably it is for that reason--together with Huxley-Murfin's
skillful handling of situation and dialogue, and the visual interpretation of the script--that the film was successful.

A few key sequences in the film illustrate these observations about the transformational skills of Huxley and Murfin.
The first few pages--or minutes--of a work are crucial in
establishing the dramatic situation and grabbing the reader
or viewer's attention. Austen's novel begins with the well-
known line, "It is a truth universally acknowledged that a
single man in possession of a good fortune must be in want
of a wife"[23] (a good example of the kind of generality which
film cannot translate). Chapter 1 goes on to establish through
flighty Mrs. Bennet's conversation at home with beleaguered
Mr. Bennet that her main concern is to get her daughters
married off; that the newly-arrived-in-town, rich Mr. Bingley
is a good catch; and that Mr. Bennet ought to do something
about it. Now, Jerome's stage adaptation follows the novel
very closely in this and the next scenes regarding the Bennets' anticipations about Bingley. [24] But the opening of the
film version is quite different from these.

There is an earlier screenplay version of Pride and
Prejudice by Zoë Akins (dated 4-8-37 and labeled "temporary
complete")[25] which also departs from Austen's beginning, but
in a different way. Akins' first scene has a young girl arriving at a tavern to see Mr. Wickham, her betrothed; however, she has come to break off the engagement (they were
to elope in four hours) as her brother had bid her to do.
This is a dramatization of the unfortunate relationship between
Darcy's innocent young sister Georgiana and the unscrupulous
fortune-hunter Wickham, which in Austen is only vaguely described in Darcy's letter to Elizabeth (Chapter 12, page 172).
Akins' second scene cuts to the soldiers' barracks at Meryton,
where Wickham is to be made an officer. He is presented to
the Bennet ladies, who find him charming--including Mrs.
Bennet, and Lydia (with whom he will later run off, as we
know). Soon, the carriage with Bingley and Darcy goes by,
noticed with curiosity by the Bennets; and so on. We see
that these scenes set up right away the contradiction between

appearance and reality, in the case of Wickham's character
(although at this point the viewer may not realize the exact
meaning of the juxtaposition).

An entirely different approach is taken in the Huxley-
Murfin script (dated 1-11-40, with changes dated as late as
3-26-40),[26] one which demonstrates immediately the various
temperaments of Mrs. Bennet and her daughters, as well as
showing the kind of society to which they belong. It is the
manners and foibles of this society (the aristocrat and near-
aristocrat), concerned with the business of getting married
to the right person, which Austen is satirizing. These first
several scenes are original with Huxley-Murfin, yet are faith-
ful to Austen's world, and form a graphic representation of
what is behind Mrs. Bennet's conversation with her husband
in the first few pages of the novel. The film begins with
Mrs. Bennet, Jane, and Elizabeth in the Meryton village
draper's shop, selecting material for dresses to be worn to
the Assembly Ball. Now they are interrupted by the clatter
of a carriage going by and Mrs. Bennet finds out that it carries the eligible new tenant and his guest at Netherfield Park,
Mr. Bingley and Mr. Darcy. Then Lady Lucas and her daughter Charlotte appear on the scene and talk with Mrs. Bennet--
evincing immediate competition in the husband-hunt. Soon
Mrs. Bennet collects her other daughters: flirty Lydia and
Kitty at a Punch and Judy show with the officers Wickham
and Denny, and pseudo-intellectual Mary in a bookstore (the
minor roles of Kitty and Mary had been eliminated in the stage
adaptation). Next a race ensues between the Bennet carriage
and the Lucas carriage to see who can get home first to ini-
tiate a social event with the newly arrived young men--again
an incident original with the screenwriters, but one which
illustrates perfectly the competitiveness in the race to make
a good marriage which will ensure social status and financial
security.

At the Bennet home there is a wonderful conversation:

> MR. BENNET (patiently): "Mrs. Bennet, for the
> thousandth time, this estate was entailed when I in-
> herited it. It must go by law to a male heir--a male
> heir, Mrs. Bennet--and as you possibly remember,
> we have no son."

> MRS. BENNET: "All the more reason why you should

take some responsibility about getting husbands for
them. But you escape into your unintelligible books
and leave all that to me. Look at them! Five of
them--without dowries! What's to become of them?"

MR. BENNET: "Yes, what is to become of the
wretched creatures? Perhaps we should have drowned
some of them at birth!"

While the fact of the entailment is given in a narrative description in Austen (Chapter 7, page 25), this conversation is original with the screenwriters. Yet Mr. Bennet's comments are
in keeping with Austen's depiction of his ironic nature; fur-
thermore, he has been irresponsible in raising his children,
and in providing for them financially. Having five daughters
--and all of them except Elizabeth as silly as his wife--was
rather a burden.

It is the Assembly Ball sequence, however, which best
demonstrates the adroit way in which the screenwriters have
used the contrapuntal elements of situation and dialogue in
Austen's novel (as Huxley had experimented with in Point
Counter Point), and enhanced them by the film's visual signifiers. With a mobile camera which dollies and tracks here
and there around the ballroom, roving from couple to couple,
and framing them in different ways suggestive of their relationships, the film treatment vividly enacts what could only
be sketchily described in Austen. Similarly, the film here
far outshines Jerome's adaptation, which by the limitations of
the stage was transformed into being a ball at the Bennets',
where we only hear the music coming from the ballroom nearby,
and instead see various couples in conversation as they enter
the living room to get some punch, and leave. The film does
have in common with the stage play the rearranging and con-
densing of several episodes scattered throughout Austen's
novel, into one event: the ball.

The novel's dance movement, with its diverging and
converging lines, has been seen as a structural device, a
kind of ritual order, by David Daiches, who commented on
the metaphor:

It is a stately dance on the lawn, but all around
there are the dark trees, the shadows.... We are
never allowed to forget ... what a serious business
this dancing is. One false step can be fatal.[27]

One false step and one's future can change from rosy to dim, if the "right" marriage is not made, or if none at all occurs. Examining this dance motif as it has been translated to the screen by the writers, and enhanced by the film's plastic images for things and movements which Austen only suggests, George Bluestone has pointed out:

> There is hardly a dramatic and psychological relation-
> ship in either the film or novel's opening events
> which is not realized here in terms of a dance re-
> lationship.[28]

How does this dance relationship work, and what have Huxley and Murfin done with it? The film version combines into one smooth dance sequence various of the novel's elements: the Assembly Ball of Chapter 3, where the haughty Darcy does not deign to dance with Elizabeth; the gathering at Netherfield in Chapter 10 where spirited Elizabeth refuses Darcy a dance to the piano music; the private ball at Nether-field in Chapter 18 where Elizabeth, taken by surprise, finally does dance with Darcy. This ball Wickham will not attend, in order to avoid Darcy, and yet the film (and play) version has him there, unpleasantly encountering Darcy (as in Chapter 15), as well as complaining about him (as in Chapter 16) while he dances with Elizabeth (a dance not found in Austen).

These dance relationships are analogues for the psychological relationships among the characters--such as Elizabeth's and Darcy's misunderstanding of one another, and themselves, until they gradually come to realize their true natures (which are actually very much alike), and learn to do the "dance." Hence, Darcy's pride (and prejudice) in at first refusing to dance with--that is, understand--Elizabeth. A comparison of dialogue here is revealing: in the novel (and the play), Darcy remarks to Bingley about Elizabeth (who is presumably out of earshot, but nonetheless overhears), "She is tolerable; but not handsome enough to tempt me; and I am in no humour at present to give consequence to young ladies who are slighted by other men" (Chapter 1, page 12). In the film the last part is changed to: "I'm in no humour tonight to give conse-quence to the middle classes at play," which changes the di-rection of his snobbery from Elizabeth as an "unpopular" woman, to her as a representative of a class beneath his. Eventually he will find that she has as much "class" as he. In the film there is also Elizabeth's refusal to dance with

Darcy when he finally asks, and her dancing off with Wickham: a double insult to Darcy. In this incident we see a visual enactment of her interior misjudging of the character of both men: she thinks Darcy despicable, and Wickham--whom she believes maltreated by Darcy--honorable; an exact reversal of their true natures. Hence, her "prejudice." In time she will learn the truth about them, and herself.

Other relationships enacted at the dance--such as Bingley dancing with Jane, Wickham dancing with Lydia (original with the film script), and Charlotte Lucas hinting at her insecurities in the social game while she and Elizabeth sit out a dance (which causes Elizabeth to comment, "Oh, why is England cursed with so many more women than men!")--all suggest what is in fact to transpire. Bingley and Jane will marry, Wickham and Lydia will run off together and eventually be made to marry (through the intervention of Darcy). And Charlotte will marry William Collins, who, despite the fact that he stands to inherit the Bennet money, and has Lady Catherine de Bourgh as patron, is an insufferably pompous bore (a marriage which idealistic--and realistic--Elizabeth considers a moral surrender on Charlotte's part).

So Huxley's Pride and Prejudice was created through a skillful use of situation and dialogue from Austen, complemented by those of his own invention. M-G-M was pleased with Huxley's work, and assured him they would always have assignments for him. Maria talked about this in a letter, saying it was "not just niceness on their part"; rather, "It's because Aldous has learnt to do their kind of thing extremely well, as he does anything he really wants to."[29] An achievement greater than that of a mere costume drama or period piece, the film is an interpretation of the ironic wit of Jane Austen, who, in her depiction of psychological states, and the need to discover our true values and selves amid the conventions and snares of society, was really rather modern.

Love Among the Ruins: "Jane Eyre"

At the time Pride and Prejudice was being released in August 1940, Huxley began writing the biography of Father Joseph, the associate of Cardinal Richelieu--a subject which reflected Huxley's continuing interest in mysticism and morality,

religion and politics. Yet as he finished Grey Eminence in
May 1941, he realized it was not the kind of book likely to
become a bestseller, and he thought about movie work again
to supplement his income. His agent Leland Hayward was
able to get him an assignment with Twentieth Century-Fox
to do an adaptation based on a book which in its own way had
a lot to do with religion and morality: Charlotte Brontë's
Jane Eyre. By the time Hollywood was finished with it, it
had a lot less to do with either.

Huxley started the assignment in July 1941, alone at
first but eventually in collaboration with John Houseman and
the film's director Robert Stevenson; these three received
screenplay credit. There is evidence that others had a hand
in it: Ketti Frings contributed to screenplay construction;
more notably, according to a studio publicity release, Orson
Welles also worked on the script.[30] The influence of Welles
is strong in Jane Eyre, extending beyond his performance as
Edward Rochester. The film's mise-en-scène suggests that of
Welles' own films Citizen Kane (1941) and The Magnificent Am-
bersons (1942), in its deep-focus photography, low-key or
chiaroscuro lighting, tracking camera shots, and overlapping
dialogue. The same is true of the acting style, and the use
of his Mercury Theatre company, such as Agnes Moorehead,
producer John Houseman, and composer Bernard Herrmann.
It is likely that Huxley's intentions and accomplishments, as
far as the screenplay was concerned, were affected or altered
by the shadow of Welles' influence.

Huxley had met the film's producer William Goetz in 1940,
through some long and fruitless negotiations for Frieda Lawrence regarding the dramatization and potential filming of D. H.
Lawrence's Lady Chatterley's Lover. Hungarian dramatist
Melchior Lengyel (known, among other things, for the original
story on which Ernst Lubitsch's Ninotchka was based in 1939)
had written a play which both Frieda and Goetz had found
unsatisfactory. Could Huxley help? He suggested Christopher
Isherwood and W. H. Auden; she asked Samuel Beckett; none
of these ended up doing the play, nor could John Van Druten
(who would later dramatize Isherwood's "Sally Bowles" from
Berlin Stories into I Am a Camera with Julie Harris in 1951).
After much correspondence and negotiation, the right playwright for the Lawrence work was never found.[31]

William Goetz also produced for Twentieth Century-Fox

an unusual trailer entitled Three Sisters of the Moors, which
was released in January 1944, the month before Jane Eyre
came out, and was clearly intended to prime the pump for
that movie. Huxley does not seem to have had anything to
do with this trailer, but it should have suited him, given
his illustrious line of Victorian ancestors (including T. H.
Huxley, Thomas Arnold, and Mrs. Humphry Ward). The
short film introduced to audiences an interesting array of
characters: the Reverend Brontë (played by Sir Cedric
Hardwicke), the Brontë sisters Charlotte, Emily, and Anne,
and others including "a Reader," "a Bookseller," Dickens,
Thackeray, and Mrs. Gaskell.[32]

Of Huxley's personal feelings about his involvement in
Jane Eyre (which lasted until April 1942), we have two views.
First, from a letter from Maria Huxley to Sybille Bedford:

> Aldous, poor Aldous is making a little urgently
> needed money at the Fox studios ... he is correct-
> ing proofs [of Grey Eminence] which come in like
> punishment. And that combined with the movie work
> is a lot for him. But this time he is doing some sort
> of nonsense for Fox and Fox is nice. They don't
> expect him to go there and sit everyday, so our life
> is much as ever.[33]

Both of them would be glad that Aldous could work at home,
which he preferred; it was Maria who would have to drive
him from Pacific Palisades to the studio (the commute would
certainly have been more difficult after April 1942 when for
health reasons they moved to a radically different environment: Llano, a tiny desert community north of Los Angeles).
We see that money was a prime consideration in his taking
the film assignment--but what about Maria's calling it "non-
sense"?

Huxley himself commented in a letter on this aspect
(keep in mind that his work dragged on for almost a year):

> have ... been working at the adaptation of a story
> for the movies--tiresome work, but unavoidable,
> since books at the moment don't keep wolves very
> far from doors, and the movie work is on the whole
> preferable to the continual shallow improvising of
> articles and stories, which is the practical alternative
> to it.[34]

Even though he allows that writing for movies is superior
work to writing for magazines, Huxley seems to be equating
both with hack work; his true métier was books--whether
fiction or non-fiction. Or perhaps he was merely being realistic. It was hard to have the "art of the screenplay"
given the facts of the Hollywood system: the studio controlled its writers through enforced script collaboration and
frequent rewrites; films were a business, to be geared towards the taste of the mass audience in order to gain the
largest profits. Huxley knew all this, yet we know that as
a professional he put great effort into his film work, as he
did with everything. His compatriot Christopher Isherwood
had something to say on this subject of writers and the movies. Upon his arrival in Los Angeles in the summer of 1939,
he met and became friends with Huxley through Gerald Heard,
and also took on movie work, obtained through Salka Viertel's
influence with Gottfried Reinhardt, a producer at M-G-M (Isherwood's screen credits include Rage in Heaven, 1941; Forever and a Day, 1944; The Loved One, 1965, and many others). Isherwood commented in an interview years later:

> "It's really almost impossible for anybody who has
> the right to call himself an artist to do second-rate
> work deliberately. People who do that kind of thing
> are really not professionals. They're just amateurs
> and then they moan over it and say, 'I'm a whore'
> or something. I have no time for that. Why don't
> you just get on with the job? If you get good
> money, why you give good value for it, and if they
> don't see the value, well that's their loss and not
> yours."[35]

It is likely that Huxley would have shared this view.

The casting of Jane Eyre had an enormous impact on
both the script and the screen. To a large extent, these
personalities (along with the film's visual style, of course)
account for a striking distinction between the screenplay as
text and the film as text. The film was originally conceived
by David O. Selznick as a vehicle for Joan Fontaine and was
later sold to Twentieth Century-Fox. Now, while the meek
and mild Fontaine was right in Selznick's production of Rebecca in 1940 (director Alfred Hitchcock's first American film,
itself an echo of Jane Eyre), she was ill-suited to play Brontë's
heroine. Fontaine's self-effacing manner does little justice to

the strong-willed Jane which emerges from the novel; what is
more, Fontaine's performance does not match up with Peggy
Ann Garner's spirited portrayal of Jane as a young girl at
Gateswood Hall and Lowood School. Fontaine's performance is
countered by the baroque acting style of Orson Welles, who
creates a wild-eyed, Byronic Rochester (a persona which
dominates her as Laurence Olivier never did in Rebecca).
Sometimes overdone, Welles' brooding and often bravura performance set against a gloomy Thornfield Hall serves to emphasize the Gothic aspects of the novel. What emerges is a
romantic melodrama with tinges of film noir.

A more recent version of Jane Eyre by Delbert Mann
in 1971 (starring Susannah York and George C. Scott) downplays these elements of Gothicism and melodrama, emphasizing
instead the psychological and spiritual growth of Brontë's
characters. This is a very different film, the sort of film we
might guess Huxley would have preferred, given his commitment to the value of self-examination and the actualization of
one's best potentialities (as he would say)--had not the constraints of Hollywood interferred. This is not to say that
director Stevenson's Jane Eyre is not a good film--cinematically
it is very interesting--only that it achieves an effect different
from Charlotte Brontë's (thus, it is an intriguing interpretation).

Now for Huxley's (we will call it that for brevity's sake)
screenplay of Jane Eyre. Coincidentally, Helen Jerome had
adapted this classic for the stage in 1936 (starring Katharine
Hepburn), omitting the early childhood scenes; Huxley did
not use Jerome's work as he did her version of Pride and
Prejudice. His screenplay follows Charlotte Brontë's novel
rather closely, except for a bit of temporal rearrangement in
the opening. This opening was in fact omitted from the release version of the film. A comparison between the two beginnings is instructive. The shooting script (marked "Revised
Final," dated 2-2-43 but with changes dated as late as 3-20-
43) begins with this instruction:

> Unless otherwise noted the CAMERA represents Jane.
> All characters speak directly into the camera as
> though they were talking to Jane. We never see
> her but on several occasions we see her hands just
> as her own eyes would see them.[36]

This directive on the use of subjective camera suggests a
technique used often by Welles (not to mention Hitchcock);
here it was obviously intended to approximate the novel's
first-person narrative, life seen from Jane's point of view.
If this technique had been used consistently throughout the
film (it was not), the effect would have been much like Robert
Montgomery's film version of Raymond Chandler's Lady in the
Lake in 1946: disastrous. For in that film, the extended
use of subjective camera, though intriguing in theory, has
the paradoxical effect of distancing the viewer from the main
character (played by Robert Montgomery)--because, except
for an occasional glimpse of him in a mirror, we cannot see
him.

The opening shots of the Jane Eyre script are a series
of dissolves up to the window of Thornfield Hall--certainly a
reminder of, if not an homage to, the beginning of Citizen
Kane (where in a succession of dissolves the probing camera
--and viewer--approaches and enters the window at Xanadu).
The script then proceeds to treat in a stylized manner Jane's
departure from Thornfield Hall and her wanderings. Next it
presents a lengthy flashback dramatizing the events leading
up to that time, then continues the story to its conclusion.

The script's opening was not used in the release version
of the film, which follows a chronological plan and begins by
showing the image of a page in a book, which is read by
Jane as a voice-over narration (a form of exposition which is
used throughout the film to introduce each sequence, or
"chapter," reminding us that the film is derived from literature):

> "My name is Jane Eyre--I was born in 1820, a harsh
> time of change in England. Money and position
> seemed all that mattered--charity was a cold and
> disagreeable word--religion too often wore a mask
> of bigotry and cruelty. There was no proper place
> for the poor or the unfortunate. I had no father or
> mother, brother or sister. As a child I lived with
> my aunt, Mrs. Reed of Gateshead Hall. I do not
> remember that she ever spoke one kind word to
> me...."

The next image on the screen is a mysterious one, showing a lit candle moving through darkness; we find this to be

held by the footman, accompanied by the servant Bessie,
coming through a corridor at Gateshead Hall to fetch Jane out
of a dark, ominous room (called the "red-room" in the novel)
where she had been locked up for punishment. She is taken
to the bright drawing room to face her harsh aunt (played
by Agnes Moorehead) and the hypocritically pious Rev. Brocklehurst, headmaster of Lowood Institution for Orphans. They
discuss how "wicked" Jane is (her sins mainly consisting of
defending herself against the torments of Mrs. Reed's spoiled
son; indeed, against the torments of her lonely life in general). She is to be sent to Lowood the next morning; for
Jane it is a welcome escape. As she leaves, she bitterly de-
nounces her aunt's ill-treatment of her, and claims her need
for love. Thus the film has effectively condensed the inci-
dents of the first five chapters of Brontë's novel. The way
this has been filmed reinforces the content. The low camera
angles from Jane's point of view emphasize her helplessness;
the high camera angles from others' point of view enforce
their power over her. Cinematically, the juxtaposition of
darkness and light forms an important visual design in the
film, with symbolic significance, as Michael Riley has so rightly
pointed out:

> Throughout the film there is a movement from dark-
> ness toward the natural light when, Gateshead long
> behind her, Jane eventually stands with Rochester
> in the burned ruins of Thornfield, its roof literally
> torn off to let in the light.[37]

But Jane must first endure more darkness at Lowood,
where Brocklehurst introduces her as an evil liar. This next
sequence skillfully compresses her difficult years there (though
it makes a few minor changes). While Jane finds a brief
friendship--and a lesson in virtue--in Helen Burns (Elizabeth
Taylor), who will die from illness induced by Brocklehurst's
cruelty, missing from the film is the one other person at Lowood who has any sympathy: Miss Temple. In her place the
film invents kindly Dr. Rivers, who helps Jane to see that
even though she hates it there after Helen's death, she must
stay at the school to get an education, if she is to do good
work in the world. Dr. Rivers is also to take the place of
another Brontë character the film omits, who is very important
to Jane's moral development later: St. John Rivers.

The Gateshead and Lowood sequences are very effective

cinema, both dramatically and visually. The remainder of
the film deals with Jane's taking on her duties as governess
at Thornfield Hall and her turbulent relationship with Rochester. The interaction of the Fontaine-Welles personalities gives
the film a somewhat different tone from the earlier segments.
The way they first meet out on the moors at night, Jane
walking and Rochester on horseback, each surprising the
other, is treated slightly differently in the film than in the
novel. As Riley incisively describes it,

> When in the novel Rochester's horse falls on the ice,
> it is nature herself bringing him down; in the film
> Jane causes the fall, foreshadowing her impact on
> him. [38]

While Jane will find Rochester "proud, sardonic and
harsh," she will also realize that "beneath the harsh mask he
assumed, lay a tortured soul, fine, gentle and kindly"--ac-
cording to Jane's voice-over. Deep calls to deep (something
the Fontaine and Welles performances are not always able to
convey); he will find in her his match at last. And in car-
ing for Rochester's ward Adele, Jane will be able to give un-
selfishly the love that was so long denied her in her own
youth. We see this in an exchange between Rochester and
Jane after he has revealed to her Adele's illegitimate birth,
and has supposed that Jane may wish to leave out of a sense
of propriety. But it only makes Jane care more for Adele.
In the novel she replies, justly,

> "No: Adele is not answerable for her mother's faults
> or yours; I have a regard for her, and now that I
> know she is, in a sense, parentless--forsaken by
> her mother and disowned by you, sir--I shall cling
> closer to her than before." [39]

In the film, this conversation is expanded and is placed after
Jane has saved Rochester from the fire mysteriously set in
his room, which emphasizes the close identification of Adele,
Jane, and Rochester as beings who need the saving power
of love:

> JANE: "Adele has had so little love, I shall try to
>   make up for it."
>
> ROCHESTER: "Are you always drawn to the loveless
>   and unfriended?"

> JANE: "When it's deserved."
>
> ROCHESTER: "Would you say that my life deserved saving?"
>
> JANE: "I should be distressed if harm came to you, sir."

Although Jane and Rochester are not equals socially, they are kindred spirits, and equal as humans, as the novel makes clear. But the film (enforced by Welles' dominant acting style) somewhat diminishes this important concept. While Rochester enjoys parrying with Jane (who secretly loves him), it does take him a while--delayed by his dalliance with the insipid Blanche Ingram--to admit to himself and to Jane that he loves her, and wants to marry her. The film omits the episode in the novel (Chapters 18 and 19) when Rochester disguises himself as a gypsy fortune teller and tells the ladies' fortunes at Thornfield--Blanche's and Jane's in particular. He uses this opportunity to talk more intimately with Jane, though she will penetrate his disguise. Interestingly, Huxley also had a similar fortune-telling scene with a man disguised as a gypsy woman in his early novel Crome Yellow, which he admitted he "borrowed, with modifications," from Jane Eyre.[40]

Rochester's proposal is really precipitated when Jane, thinking he is to marry Blanche, has an outburst. In the film Jane's highly self-revelatory speech matches that in the novel almost word for word:

> "Do you think I could stay here to become nothing to you? Do you think because I'm poor and obscure and plain that I'm soulless and heartless? I have as much soul as you, and fully as much heart. And if God had gifted me with wealth and beauty, I should've made it as hard for you to leave me as it is now for me to leave you."

That speech in the film omits Jane's next remark and Rochester's reply to her which we find in the novel (Ch. 23, p. 190):

> "I am not talking to you now through the medium of custom, conventionalities, or even of mortal flesh: --it is my spirit that addresses your spirit; just as

        if both had passed through the grave, and we stood
        at God's feet, equal,--as we are!"
        "As we are!" repeated Mr. Rochester.

Thus in the novel Rochester admits both his love and his
equality with Jane; in the film, his reply (a line actually taken
from later in the novel) expresses something else:

        "Jane, Jane, you strange, you, yes, almost unearthly
        thing--you that I love as my own flesh!"

    By omitting that last exchange in the novel, the film
here (and elsewhere) not only downplays the idea of "equality," but virtually eliminates the religious and moral underpinnings of the novel. While the novel is a love story, it is
more than that. It is also the story of spiritual education--
primarily that of Jane; and she in turn is responsible for
helping Rochester. These spiritual considerations are not
entirely missing from the film; for example, Rochester will
mutter "God pardon me" (as in the novel) when Jane agrees
to marry him, indicating some awareness of his transgression.
Yet the film reduces the spiritual and moral implications of the
story for the sake of simplicity, casting, and box office. Its
theme is epitomized in its overblown publicity slogan: "A Love
Story Every Woman Would Die a Thousand Deaths to Live!"[41]

    All of which leads to the next important point about
Jane's relationship with Rochester, encompassing her moral
duty to him, and to herself. As the couple are about to be
wed, the service is interrupted by the announcement that
Rochester already has a wife living. He confirms this by
revealing that it is his insane wife who is the mysterious,
laughing, evil presence of the upper floor at Thornfield.
Now Jane faces a moral dilemma: she cannot marry Rochester
(whom she had loved to the point of idolatry), and she will
not stay to be his mistress, or his "comforter," his "rescuer,"
as Rochester beseeches her. She must flee. This is where
the film departs from the novel in a crucial way. In the
novel, her wanderings lead her to the house of a zealous
clergyman, St. John Rivers, who helps her and obtains a
teaching position for her. Impressed with her character,
Rivers proposes that she marry him to help him with his
missionary work. But this would be a marriage without love,
just as immoral as Rochester's offer of love without marriage.
She realizes this as she considers the situation--and suddenly
senses Rochester calling her. She must go to see him.

The film, however, eliminates the St. John Rivers episode, and instead has Jane flee to Gateshead, where she finds
her aunt ill (which makes use of a similar episode found earlier in the novel). Soon a solicitous Dr. Rivers (whom we
have met earlier in the film at Lowood) calls there, looking for
Jane, as he has received a letter from Rochester's lawyer in-
quiring after Jane's whereabouts. She would prefer him not
to answer. Her aunt dies; Jane's future is uncertain. During
a storm, while writing a letter about teaching at Lowood, she
"hears" Rochester calling her. The film in this segment is
actually different from the screenplay version, in which Dr.
Rivers' role is expanded. There, he asks Jane to be his wife
and help him with his work--which Jane refuses, saying, "I
could never marry someone I didn't love." The point to be
made here is that while this Dr. Rivers is certainly different
from the novel's St. John Rivers, in the script he does serve
a similar function in testing Jane's feelings, helping her decide her priorities, and giving her an alternative to her ques-
tionable future without Rochester. Yet by omitting this alternative relationship and Jane's decision, the release version of
the film diminishes Jane's moral examination and changes the
impact of her final reunion with Rochester.

That is, where in the novel (and to some degree in the
script) Jane finally gets together again with Rochester--who
has now lost Thornfield, his insane wife, and his eyesight--
each has matured spiritually and atoned for past errors and
sins (she for loving him more than God, he for loving her
with an encumbered heart). In the film their reunion, in the
ruins of Thornfield, is more that of lovers finally free to love
--a moving story, to be sure, but one without the fuller moral
implications with which the novel endows their reunion. The
film Jane Eyre is an effective adaptation, moving in its own
moody way, a romantic melodrama which shows respect for the
art of cinema. To speculate on what the film would have been
like had Huxley's influence been stronger, and Welles' less, is,
finally, to quibble. Rather, we should remember a principle
of film adaptation: in Welles' own words, "I believe you must
say something new about a book, otherwise it is better not to
touch it."[42]

Between Takes

During the time he had been occupied with writing the

screenplay for Jane Eyre, and while that film was being shot,
Huxley was also busy with work of his own. The Art of Seeing (1942) described his successful experience with using the
Bates Method of eye exercise. His favorite among his own
novels, Time Must Have a Stop (1944), explored further his
interest in the themes of conversion and regeneration seen
in Eyeless in Gaza and After Many a Summer Dies the Swan.
Dividing his time between his desert home in Llano and his
pied-à-terre at 145½ S. Doheny Drive in Beverly Hills, Huxley's interest in film work continued. Even his son Matthew
was smitten with the movies and found a job "working as a
reader, making synopses of books for Warner Bros." for
about a year; as Huxley described it, it was

> a job he seems to like quite well, except when he
> has to read the Ladies Home Journal and True Con-
> fessions in search of dramatic nuggets which are
> never there. [43]

Before obtaining his next screen credit with A Woman's
Vengeance, Huxley became involved with several film projects.
In the spring of 1944 he began the first of his collaborations
with Christopher Isherwood. It was a time when both writers
were immersed in studies of mysticism: Huxley was working
on The Perennial Philosophy, an anthology of the mystics
with explanatory commentary (published in 1945); Isherwood
was deeply into Vedanta, having just translated the Bhagavad-
Gita. What they came up with was an original screenplay entitled Jacob's Hands, the story of a faith healer. Huxley was
making an effort independently to write and sell a film script,
in hopes of avoiding the constraints of studio intervention.
He wrote to Frieda Lawrence about the script:

> I hope we shall be able to sell it, as it will solve a
> lot of economic problems and will make it unnecessary
> to go into temporary slavery at one of the studios. [44]

However, they were unable to find a buyer. Huxley
found out why from his agent Donald Hyde of the William Mor-
ris Agency, and wrote to Isherwood about it on July 28, 1944:

> It appears that the reason for the hitherto universal
> rejection of it is fear of the doctors.... [Yet] the
> doctors have no grounds for complaint--the healer's
> biggest medical success is a moral failure, his biggest

> moral success a medical failure, he retires from all
> but veterinary business because he feels he can't
> use his gift rightly.[45]

The script was never filmed, although it was later adapted
and broadcast on the radio. Jacob's Hands--like Huxley's
earlier unsold scenario, Success--dealt with the kind of controversial subject Hollywood was hesitant to touch, for fear
of antagonizing influential groups.

No longer was Huxley merely criticizing film as just
another product of modern technology designed to distract
the masses into passivity; now he was actively engaged in
trying to use the medium to educate people, or to heighten
their awareness of various things or issues. This desire to
utilize film's potentialities coincided with his changing attitudes
and intentions about life, as we have noted in his fiction beginning with Eyeless in Gaza, which presented a path leading
away from the horror of the Brave New World depicted four
years earlier. With Huxley's deepening interest in mysticism,
pacifism, and the need to steer the world away from its de-
structive course, his fiction changed from satirical description
to satirical exhortation. His interest in film--enhanced by his
experience in, and indeed, proximity to the medium--paralleled
that desire to enlighten.

In line with that attitude, Huxley had other ideas for
films besides Jacob's Hands. He wrote enthusiastically to
Matthew in July 1944 regarding possible films about art, "to
illustrate the technique of the various arts as well as the actual works as they have appeared in the course of history."
Etching might be demonstrated, and master works shown; or
painters or sculptors at work, a model in the background:
"This approach would interest people more than the merely
historical or aesthetic discussion of painting; for everybody
likes to know how a thing is done."[46] Apparently nothing
ever came of this idea, but it does suggest--along with his
later ideas about films on population, and the life of Gandhi,
for example--that Huxley might have been well-suited to documentary filmmaking; perhaps something similar to what his
brother Julian had done in England with films on science and
nature.

In 1945 Huxley got an assignment perfect for someone
with his direct line into Victorian literature and society, and

one which he enjoyed: he was to do the script of Alice in
Wonderland for Walt Disney. As Huxley described it to Anita
Loos in October,

> [It] is to be a cartoon version of Tenniel's drawings
> and Carroll's story, embedded in a flesh-and-blood
> episode of the life of the Rev. Charles Dodgson. I
> think something rather nice might be made out of
> this--the unutterably odd, repressed and ridiculous
> Oxford lecturer on logic and mathematics, seeking
> refuge in the company of little girls and in his own
> phantasy.[47]

The detached, scholarly type who lives more through his books
and research than through actual life is a recurrent figure in
Huxley's fiction, so Huxley was well-equipped to deal with
that sort in a film. We see the prototype in Crome Yellow's
Henry Wimbush, who understands the past better than the
present, and books better than people; his credo is "The
proper study of mankind is books." Struggling against this
creed is Denis Stone, a sensitive young man trying to get
out from under the weight of books: "One reads so many,
and one sees so few people and so little of the world."[48]
The detached scholarly or scientific type comes up again and
again in Huxley's fiction--James Shearwater in Antic Hay,
Philip Quarles in Point Counter Point, John Beavis and Hugh
Ledwidge in Eyeless in Gaza--but the character which comes
closest to that of the odd Charles Dodgson is Jeremy Pordage
in After Many a Summer Dies the Swan. Pordage, like Dodgson, escapes his ineptitudes through fantasies and girls (but
the older kind, who rent by the hour).

Huxley had some clever ideas for the Alice in Wonderland film, and took a particular interest in its background of
Victorian eccentricities--with some personal reasons, for in
fact Huxley's mother Julia Arnold had lived in Oxford as a
child, and had been photographed by Dodgson; Huxley's aunt
Mrs. Humphry Ward had also left some lively accounts of
Victorian Oxford. But Huxley came to realize that

> as usual, it turns out to be impossible to make any
> of the documentary points which it would be so amus-
> ing (at any rate for me) to elaborate.... even if
> there were time, how few of the millions who see the

film would take the smallest interest in the recon-
struction of this odd fragment of the forgotten past!
So I have to be content with bringing out as many
of the oddities of Dodgson as possible, and with pre-
venting producer and director from putting in too
many anachronisms and impossibilities for the sake
of the story. [49]

He spent several months on the project, yet sadly his material was not used. Perhaps Walt Disney found it too literary.
When released in 1951, the animated film turned out to be a
rather dull rendering of the work of Carroll and Tenniel.
It was entertaining in a silly way--the Cheshire Cat is memor-
able--but certainly a far cry from Huxley's vision of it, and
less interesting.

The other film project which came up in 1945 proved to
be a very long-term, problematic one: the adaptation of
Brave New World, to be produced by Huxley's friends Paulette
Goddard and her new husband Burgess Meredith. Discussing
the possibilities of the film in an October letter to Anita Loos,
Huxley stressed that

It is essential, I think, to anchor the brave-new-
worldian events very firmly to the present, so as to
show that even the most extravagant pieces of satiric phantasy stem inevitably and logically from
present-day seeds and are the natural end-product
of present-day tendencies. This will give the picture
a strong topical interest and will give a specific point
to its satire. [50]

Indeed, with an increasingly technological, mass society, and
with the dropping of the atomic bomb on Hiroshima on August
6, 1945, the world was coming closer to becoming the dystopia
depicted in Huxley's novel. Huxley wondered about the censors: "what will the Hays Office say about babies in bottles?"
There were many problems to be discussed later, and he
hoped that Anita would be there too, "with that dramatist's -
eye view of things, which I don't have." [51] A film or play
written by Huxley and Loos, given their compatibility, might
have been a very interesting thing indeed; they once specu-
lated on doing a new version of Oliver Goldsmith's She Stoops
to Conquer, but it never happened. [52]

Huxley reflected on writing the Brave New World screenplay--providing the negotiations were successful--to his writer friend Victoria Ocampo, editor of the literary review Sur in Buenos Aires:

> It will be interesting to see how much can be said in that medium--and how much one will be allowed to say. The fact that films cannot pay their expenses unless they are seen by twenty or thirty million people, imposes the most enormous intellectual and conventional limitations. There can be no change in the present situation until arrangements are made for exhibiting special films to a limited public, as is done with plays and with books. But this can't be done unless the cost of making films is enormously reduced.[53]

Huxley's understanding of the business of filmmaking had certainly matured; he was learning to deal with some of its frustrations in seeing his ideas through to the screen.

Negotiations fell through on the Brave New World film project, because the current owners of the dramatic rights to the book (sold to RKO in 1932 when the book was published, by Huxley's careless agent Ralph B. Pinker) would neither do the film nor let anyone else do it.[54] Although the project was off for the time being, Huxley stayed hopeful. In 1956, with the assistance of Franklin Lacey (known for The Music Man), Huxley rewrote Brave New World as a musical comedy (of all things!). His reasons? As he wrote to Matthew,

> everyone tells me that science fiction can never succeed on the stage as a straight play, but that it will be accepted when the medium ceases to be realistic and makes use of music and lyrics[55]

Huxley included here a sample song from the musical (finished by December 1956), to be sung by the "Epsilons." The last verse went like this:

> "Lots to eat and hours for drinking
> Soma cocktails--no more thinking.
> NO MORE THINKING, NO MORE THINKING!
> Everybody's happy now."[56]

However, the composer for this musical was never found (Huxley had thought of Stravinsky, had asked Leonard Bernstein) and the project was abandoned. In 1957 RKO offered to sell the rights back to Huxley, but for a sum judged to be excessive: $50,000. Finally, in 1963, the new owners at RKO sold the rights to Samuel Bronston, although Huxley never received a share of the proceeds of the sale, as he had been promised.[57] Eventually Brave New World was made as a Universal Television mini-series on NBC in 1978 (starring Julie Cobb, Bud Cort, and Keir Dullea), but the campy treatment was a travesty of Huxley's novel.

Alone at Last: "A Woman's Vengeance"

Huxley's next film project, to judge at least by the quality and number of his letters on the subject, was one which absorbed him more deeply than any other. This was because of the personal nature of the work: the film, eventually titled by Universal A Woman's Vengeance (1947), was an adaptation of Huxley's own short story, "The Gioconda Smile" (from Mortal Coils, 1922); the screenplay was to be by Huxley alone. Huxley subsequently derived a stage version, quite similar to the screenplay. So the tale of love and murder had three manifestations by Huxley, which provide a unique opportunity to judge the author's intentions and skill in various media.

This short story is one of Huxley's best pieces of work, demonstrating tight construction and a nice balance between the medium and the message. It concerns the philandering Henry Hutton, with an invalid wife, Emily. Janet Spence--an intellectual spinster of thirty-six with a mysterious, "Gioconda" smile--is in love with Henry, and secretly poisons his wife, believing that then they will be free to be together. Yet Janet is spurned by Henry, who marries a young woman, Doris, with whom he had been having an affair. Janet takes revenge by accusing him of murdering his wife, for which he is soon convicted. Henry (who had once jokingly called himself the "Christ of Ladies") comes to realize that "Experience doesn't teach"; that

   some extraordinary kind of justice was being done.

In the past he had been wanton and imbecile and
irresponsible. Now Fate was playing as wantonly,
as irresponsibly, with him. It was tit for tat, and
God existed after all.[58]

Henry is executed for the crime. But Janet--whose queer
character forms the interest of the story--is increasingly tor-
mented by guilt and sleeplessness, and she finally confesses
to Dr. Libbard. Finis.

The screenplay version makes a few modifications in the
story, reflecting Huxley's changing aesthetic and philosophical
intentions. A few characters are added to round things out;
Dr. Libbard is changed from being a complacent cynic to an
active guru (suggesting some other "saintly" Huxleyan characters, such as Dr. James Miller in Eyeless in Gaza, William
Propter in After Many a Summer, and Bruno Rontini in Time
Must Have a Stop); and the ending of the story is changed
to emphasize a different moral lesson.

Spending time at Wrightwood (his newly acquired mountain retreat), as well as Llano (in the desert, about twenty
miles away) or Beverly Hills, Huxley worked on the screenplay from July to October of 1946; in October he began the
stage version, which would take a few years to produce.
Huxley enjoyed a good working relationship with the film's
director, Zoltan Korda (who, like his brother Alexander Korda,
had been active in the British film industry in the 1930s; his
later films included Jungle Book, Sahara, and The Macomber
Affair). Korda had a respect for writers and writing; as
Huxley told Anita Loos in October,

> He is a nice, intelligent fellow and we were able to
> coordinate our respective specialities of writer and
> director without the interference of a producer.
> Consequently the work was done quickly and effi-
> ciently, without being held up by retired button-
> manufacturers using the Divine Right of Money to
> obstruct the activities of those who do the actual
> work.[59]

Later there was talk of the Korda brothers making a film of
Point Counter Point, with Huxley doing the script. It was
an arrangement he would have found quite agreeable, but
nothing more came of that idea;[60] Point Counter Point was

eventually made as a five-part television series in 1972-73 for Britain's "Masterpiece Theatre."

Meanwhile there were some revisions to be made in the "Gioconda Smile" script; but rather than trouble with the producer (who turned out to be Zoltan Korda), there was some problem with the censors of the Production Code Administration over the script as the film was being readied for production in the summer of 1947. Huxley was back at the studio in June (at $1,560 a week), "patching up the script after its mangling by the censors."[61] As Huxley wrote to Anita Loos in July,

> The censors demanded the cutting of various scenes
> --fortunately not essential ones; and the information
> they were meant to convey (about the young girl's
> pre-marital pregnancy) can be put across, not by
> honest statement, but by "becks and nods and
> wreathed smiles," the principle of the Johnston Of-
> fice's morality being that nothing may be said in a
> decent way but that all may be suggested inde-
> cently.[62]

Also in this letter we find an amusing anecdote about why they could not get Claude Raines to play the part of Dr. Libbard (the role in which Sir Cedric Hardwicke was subsequently cast):

> We failed to get Raines, as he wanted a salary raise
> and the Studio casting manager was adamant. "In
> this Studio," he told Korda, "not even Jesus Christ
> could get a raise in salary." (It would make a splen-
> did subject for a religious painting--the Saviour be-
> fore Mannix, Katz and Mayer, pleading for a hike in
> his wages, and being turned down cold.)[63]

It is all the more interesting that Huxley used this same incident in the introductory section which he added later to his novel (written between the fall of 1947 and February 1948), cast in the form of a lost screenplay, Ape and Essence. In this novel the pungent remark "'Bob,' he said, 'in this Studio, at this time, not even Jesus Christ himself could get a raise'" is then expanded into a series of imagined religious paintings of the subject "Christ before Lublin." There are wonderful descriptions of versions by Rembrandt (a turbaned figure in

the "golden spotlight"), Breughel ("A great synoptic view of
the entire Studio"), and Piero ("the composition, luminously
explicit").[64] Huxley's visual imagination, aided by his keen
appreciation of painting, here reminds one in a strange way
of the allegorical painting in Nathanael West's The Day of the
Locust--"The Burning of Los Angeles." The connection of
Los Angeles and its movie industry with some sort of apoc-
alypse in a recurrent motif in "Hollywood" novels.

As for the film, despite the difficulties posed by the
troubles with the censors and the failure to get Raines, Huxley felt that he had got his story "through the cutting rooms
without losing anything from any of the essential scenes."[65]
The film was well-acted, with Charles Boyer as Henry Maurier
(the name changed from "Hutton" to accommodate the French-
man), although there is something a bit cold about Boyer's
charm (shades of Gaslight?). Neurotic Janet is well depicted
by Jessica Tandy, playing a persona here who has about as
much eroticism as a fish. A most satisfactory character is
Hardwicke's Dr. Libbard, a mustached, tweedy, pipe-smoking
gentleman whose calm, offhanded manner enables him to exert
change in others. At the last minute the studio, believing
that most Americans wouldn't know that "Gioconda" referred
to the "Mona Lisa," decided to call the film A Woman's Vengeance (but they did allow Henry, early in the film, to bid
Janet goodbye with "Adieu, le sourire mysterieux"--which
must have been of some satisfaction to the cognoscenti).

Yet although the production of the film had gone relatively smoothly, Huxley had felt some anxiety in writing it.
As the double project of film and play progressed, Huxley had
begun to feel frustrated by the demands of the medium he was
trying to work in. In a February 1947 letter to Leon M. Lion
(who had produced Huxley's first play, The World of Light,
in London in 1931), Huxley confesses,

> It has been quite interesting as a literary problem--
> this translation and development of an old theme into
> and through two different media. But I am glad that
> the jobs are nearly finished; for I have grown tired
> of the endless jig-saw puzzle and carpentry work
> that has to go into a play and, still more, into a
> scenario.[66]

Huxley continues to reveal his feelings about dramatic writing
versus narrative:

Also, I find, one gets tired in a play of having to
express everything in terms of dialogue. This would
be all right if one were Shakespeare and could make
of every exchange, every casual reflection, something
astonishingly poetical. But not being Shakespeare,
and working in the realistic medium of the modern
play, one has to stick to conversational verisimilitude
and to be, therefore, even less poetical than one is
capable of being in narrative, where the medium per-
mits of a greater freedom in the manipulation of words
and a greater variety in the kinds of writing that it
is possible to use. [67]

The root of Huxley's resistance to the demands of dialogue
writing in drama is probably found in his difficulty in dramatizing situations creatively, as Beth Wendel, his collaborator
on The Genius and the Goddess, has said. Indeed, according
to Grover Smith, the playwright John Van Druten also made
this discovery about Huxley when he was shown an early
draft of "The Gioconda Smile" play, and he helped Huxley
revise the play--his part being kept secret at Van Druten's
request. [68] The play finally opened in London in June 1948,
and in New York, October 1950 (with Basil Rathbone and Valerie Taylor). Both were rather short runs; the play was not
as successful as the film version.

Obviously a film, unlike a play, has other means than
words to convey meaning: mise-en-scène and montage. The
director usually prefers to show us, rather than tell us; as
François Truffaut has said of Alfred Hitchcock's work, the
"rule of counterpoint between dialogue and image creates a
dramatic effect by purely visual means." [69] Zoltan Korda's
A Woman's Vengeance is a very literate film, both in its de-
pendence on words and in the intelligent quality of its dialogue. Yet it has all the Hitchcockian elements--suspense,
complacency, revenge, guilt--except the director himself.
An absorbing drama, it might have been enhanced by a director with a keener eye for visual signifiers. But let us
examine the film as Huxley wrote it, and Korda shot it.

That this will be a film about relationships of sometimes
stifling intensity is set up at the film's beginning, which
opens not with an establishing shot but rather right in the
living room of Henry's house: Henry and Emily argue over
her wanting to give a check to her no-good brother. The

treacherous situation is immediately set up in the dialogue.
Emily rants on about Henry being bored with her and her
illness, saying that he wishes she were dead, to which Henry
replies, "Oh, I certainly shall if you go on like this!"[70] His
comment is overheard by Nurse Braddock (Mildred Natwick),
who of course will recall this argument later on as incriminat-
ing evidence against Henry in the supposed murder of his
wife.

While the first scene clearly establishes Henry's difficult
domestic situation, the next sets up the circumstances from
which Janet will evolve her scheme. At the neighboring
Spence house Henry presents some gifts for Janet and her
invalid father. There are books for her, which she protests
she does not deserve, and her father then delivers a line with
more meaning than he knows: "You deserve everything you
get." There is a parallel set up between the situations of
Janet and of Henry: each must care for an invalid at home,
but the crucial difference between them is that whereas for
Janet this situation has been unhealthy, stifling her life (even
her father remarks that she's sacrificing herself to him), for
Henry his situation is not so bad because he's free to enjoy
a playboy life on the side. Janet, not knowing of his secret
life, sees a compatibility between the two of them. Henry
unknowingly encourages Janet's ideas in this direction, both
in his invitation to her to lunch the next day, and when they
talk of their mutual interest in modern painting--which she
says he awakened in her years ago. It is clear that Janet's
personality tends toward the intellectual. It is equally evident that she mistakes Henry's flirtatious charm as interest
in her; she is as blind to the real Henry as he is to the real
Janet (hence his teasing her about her mysterious smile,
which is actually the outward sign of her repressed self).
We see the real Henry when he leaves the Spence house and
jumps into the back seat of his chauffeur-driven car, in which
waits his young mistress Doris (Ann Blyth). Deeply in love
with Henry, she's jealous of Janet; he admits he flirted with
Janet, but "only spiritually." Much later, after Henry's wife
has died and he has secretly married Doris, Henry expresses
his priorities in response to Doris's worrying that she's not
on his intellectual level as Janet is: "There's more to marriage than polite conversation--that's why I married you, and
not Janet Spence."

On that fateful day of the luncheon at Henry's house,

a self-pitying Emily unwittingly confirms Janet's plans by telling her when they are alone that "I'm alive only because Henry would be so happy if I died." Unseen by anyone, Janet poisons Emily's coffee; Emily will die that night attended by Janet, who has been sent for by the maid. Dr. Libbard diagnoses the death as a heart attack, probably induced by indigestion from eating red currants at lunch, and Henry, when he finds out, will blame Nurse Braddock for allowing it. But unfortunately Henry had been out that night on an assignation with Doris. His return late that evening to find Emily dead prompts a conversation between him and Dr. Libbard, important in its revelation of the story's philosophical underpinnings. When Henry begins to say, "Shall I tell you where I was this evening?" the doctor implies that it is obvious. Although he finds Henry's way of life contemptible, he is sorry for him, for his being someone born with money and not having to work. For it is work which gives "purpose and direction to one's life"; a rich man can afford to live "discontinuously" (a fine Huxleyan word). To Henry's query, "Do you think I'm capable of changing?" the doctor replies, "At this moment, yes," but later it will be harder. For this has been Henry's character: moments of resolve to change his ways are later overcome by moments of passion. Whatever happens will not surprise the doctor, who has, as he says, stopped being surprised at anything by now. In any event this conversation is important in paving the way for Henry's conversion experience later (again, something we have seen before in Huxley--for example, the conversion of the dissolute Anthony Beavis in Eyeless in Gaza).

The dramatic turning point in the film occurs in an emotional scene when, soon after Emily's death, Janet confesses her love for Henry and expects him to reveal at last his love for her. The scene is set against the de rigueur dark stormy evening, in Henry's home. Henry's initially light banter (of the storm he remarks, "Goodness, this is like the overture from William Tell") is played against Janet's increasing passion, which parallels the mounting intensity of the storm, which she finds "a liberation." Looking outside at the heavy rain and the tree branches beating about in the strong wind, she is stirred to bare her soul: she knows what Henry's been through, she says, "isolation, spiritual loneliness." The storm--"it's wonderful. It's like passion," she muses. Henry, getting very uncomfortable by now, replies, "You've been reading too many novels." But there's no turning back now

for Janet: "Henry--we're free now! We needn't pretend any
longer." At this climactic point she has come over and knelt
beside Henry's chair, their faces closer than at any other
point in the film, framed in a tight two-shot. Henry must
break the spell: "You don't understand...." Realizing the
truth finally, Janet can only say, as she moves away from
him, "Please forgive me." But when Henry decides to tell
her that he has married young Doris, this is the final blow;
Janet is absolutely dumbstruck, can only laugh strangely.
She then pretends that the whole scene she had just made
was only a joke--"You didn't think me serious, did you?"
But she was deadly serious. Here in this encounter are
planted the seeds of a woman's vengeance. If she cannot
have him, she'll see to it that no one else can.

Resentment at being made a scapegoat in Emily's
death will lead Nurse Braddock to implicate Henry as the one
who poisoned Emily when he gave her her medicine at lunch
(indeed the nurse gives the film some vitriolic humor, as the
idea of Henry's philandering provokes her to sharp comments
on men: "Sex! All they think about!" and "I wouldn't trust
any of them! Pigs!"). Janet goes along with the nurse's
accusation (so convenient) and seizes the opportunity to get
back at Henry for spurning her. The body is exhumed and
found to show arsenic poisoning. Henry is called back from
his honeymoon in Paris and brought to trial, where others
give damaging testimony of his character. "All his follies
coming back to him," as Dr. Libbard remarks to Janet. Finally he is convicted on circumstantial evidence and sentenced
to die. The real dramatic interest of the film lies in its last
third, which cuts between showing what Henry is going
through in jail, and what Janet, herself a prisoner of her
own guilt, is going through at home. Dr. Libbard, who has
been treating her for anxiety and insomnia, suspects Janet
as the culprit; he never thought Henry guilty of the murder.
The last part of the film is a showdown: can Dr. Libbard
get a confession out of Janet, who is beginning to crack under the strain, in time to save Henry from execution?

The final sequences of the film are especially important,
both in demonstrating Huxley's skills at maintaining suspense
and in revealing his intentions as to the "message" of the film.
In evaluating the film's handling of suspense we might pause
for a moment to consider some observations by Hitchcock which
seem tailor-made to the circumstances of A Woman's Vengeance:

> Sequences can never stand still; they must carry
> the action forward, just as the wheels of a ratchet
> mountain railway move the train up the slope, cog
> by cog. A film cannot be compared to a play or
> novel. It is closer to a short story, which, as a
> rule, sustains one idea that culminates when the
> action has reached the highest point of the dramatic
> curve.... a short story is rarely put down in the
> middle, and in this sense it resembles a film. And
> it is because of this peculiarity that there must be
> a steady development of the plot and the creation of
> gripping situations which must be presented, above
> all, with visual skill. Now, this brings us to sus-
> pense, which is the most powerful means of holding
> on to the viewer's attention.[71]

A Woman's Vengeance enjoys the status of being based
on a short story, but how well does it conform to Hitchcock's
exhortation? The last four scenes of the film contrive to balance suspense with philosophy. First, Janet comes to visit
Henry in jail, talking with him through the barred window
of his cell. He expresses the wish that "one could believe
in justice"; she asserts that there is justice. She begins to
rave, accusing him of playing with her, taunting him. Henry
stares at her, astonished at her bizarre behavior, then suddenly realizes that it was she who killed Emily, and goes ber-
serk, shouting the truth to the guards, who ignore it and
restrain him. Besides the dramatic intensity, the interesting
thing about this scene is the way it is shot--in a series of re-
verse-angle one-shots with Janet's face framed behind the
bars, and Henry's face without the bars, indicating the true
nature of things.

The next scene takes place on the following day--the
day of the execution--at Janet's house. Dr. Libbard is probing a markedly nervous Janet with a bit of indirect psychology. He tells her, you know the reason Emily was unhappy
was that she "wouldn't accept the facts as she found them";
but it is "possible to come to terms with even the most terrible facts." Continuing to reflect, he points out the price
of feeling guilty: if one runs away, one runs into "madness
and death," but if one faces it, there's a good chance to
escape this fate. Janet says she'll think about it. While
she goes to get them some drinks, the suspense builds as
Dr. Libbard secretly sets the clock ahead an hour; as she

hands him his drink, we wonder is she poisoning him too because he knows too much? The thought has occurred to him
also; he intentionally spills his drink, so that he must get
another one. He continues the conversation, dropping a bomb-
shell when he comments that killing Emily was "like murdering
a dead woman," since she only had a few months to live anyway. Janet is shocked, and breaks into a nervous laugh.
The joke is on her.

We now cut to Henry in his jail cell, where he is being
visited by Doris. They discuss names for the baby she is
expecting. Henry is now a changed man from the previous
day's encounter with Janet. Overnight he must have done
a lot of thinking, for now he has faced the facts and accepted
them--thus putting into practice Dr. Libbard's advice. There
is a sense of resolve about Henry now, and he proceeds to
indulge in some philosophizing to Doris. He has realized that
"We can't understand life while we're actually living it";
rather, we must live it forward, understand it backward.
Presumably having meditated on his own past transgressions,
he has come to accept the injustice perpetrated on him. However, he will not reveal the truth about Janet to Doris, except
to tell her not to see her anymore. Henry affirms his love to
Doris, and his realization that "love casts out fear"; it works
the other way too--"fear casts out love." Even with this
moralizing, the teacher in Huxley has not overcome the artist; the scene works.

The clincher comes in the final scene back at Janet's,
where, playing cards, she and Dr. Libbard wait out the time
of the execution, with Janet imagining what Henry is going
through. Suspense builds. Will she crack? As the clock
strikes the hour, indicating the time of the execution, Janet
becomes hysterical. Soothing her, the doctor says, "It's all
right now ... let yourself go ... you're safe now." He gives
her an injection of a sedative. He can now ask, "How did
you poison her?" "In the coffee," she replies, drifting to
sleep. The doctor calls the governor to stay the execution
--in plenty of time, since he had set the clock ahead. Justice will prevail after all.

The question is, do the film's last four scenes, with
their shifting back and forth between Henry and Janet, work
as drama, and maintain suspense? Yes, because cinema permit things which might not work on stage. In fact, Huxley's

play version of "The Gioconda Smile" used a double stage for
the final scenes, which seemed to work against itself, according to one theatre critic:

> ... Huxley ruined his last act or rather robbed it
> of a great deal of its effect. Twice when he had
> his audience nicely gripped he broke the tension by
> switching across to the prison cell and showing us
> how the condemned man was behaving under the
> threat of being executed for a crime he had not
> committed.... [He] here called upon his audience
> to think at a moment when he had worked it up to
> such a pitch that its only desire was to feel.[72]

The sequence works, however, in the film. A remark
by André Bazin on "Theater and Cinema" (from What Is Cinema?) has a certain application here:

> If by cinema we understand liberty of action in re-
> gard to space, and freedom to choose your angle of
> approach to the action, then filming a play should
> give the setting a breadth and reality unattainable
> on the stage. It would also free the spectator from
> his seat and by varying the shots give an added
> quality to the acting.[73]

Whereas drama exists in "real time," film has the ability to
shorten or lengthen time. As Hitchcock put it, "there's no
relation whatever between real time and filmic time";[74] therefore, the shifting of scenes becomes plausible in the film.
Secondly, since film, unlike drama, achieves its meaning
through montage as well as visual style, the juxtaposition of
these final scenes enacts the final irony of Henry's gradual
enlightenment set against Janet's decline. As Huxley described
it,

> the story has been developed in such a way that the
> man who is falsely condemned for his wife's murder
> ... finds an internal solution by the acceptance of
> his fate, while the woman who actually did commit
> the murder and who seems to have successfully got
> away with it, refuses to accept the real state of
> things and thus breaks down into madness.[75]

There is a certain power to A Woman's Vengeance,

particularly at the end, with the trenchant acting of Jessica
Tandy as Janet and Cedric Hardwicke as Dr. Libbard, as they
are locked in a battle of minds, indeed, of principles. Huxley's script was competent in this, his only solo screen credit,
and the only film which allowed him the opportunity to set
forth some of his own philosophy of enlightenment.

CHAPTER III. "HOLLYWOOD" NOVELS

The Writer In Hollywood

Previous chapters have explored some of Huxley's earlier writing efforts in view of his ideas about film, as well as his contributions to film as a screenwriter and adapter. But there is another side of the subject to be examined--not only Huxley's work in film, but the impact of that work on his own writing. The interactions between film and literature in Huxley's later writing career can be best understood by studying the two novels which more than any others reflect his direct reactions to what was radically new in his life--the environment of southern California, and the medium of film: After Many a Summer Dies the Swan, and Ape and Essence.

In turning to these novels, we need to keep a few things in mind. First, Huxley was a prolific writer--of fiction and non-fiction--both before and during his California residency. With his temperament, and his diverse interests and acquaintances, Huxley never found Hollywood "inimical to writing," as had Anthony Powell. Nor did he ever complain about it as had Nathanael West (who yet managed to achieve a small masterpiece about the underside of Hollywood: The Day of the Locust). When asked if he could "really" write there, West replied,

> I'll be writing, but a writer needs to lead a writer's life. It isn't just a sitting down--it's the whole business of thinking and reverie and walking and reading, and you can't do that in Hollywood, so I don't know what my future will be. But I'm going to be working. [1]

Huxley managed "thinking and reverie and walking and reading"

very well in Los Angeles, which perhaps proves something
more about personality than geography. The change in Huxley's fiction after the watershed of Eyeless in Gaza was ef-
fected by his moving to California and his subsequent film
work, as well as by his emerging philosophy and artistic intentions begun in the mid-1930s, that is, the shift from an
emphasis on aesthetics to one on mysticism and morality; his
turning from the role of writer as artist to writer as teacher.
But the bizarre quality of these novels is certainly based on
his Hollywood experience.

Which leads to the second point. Huxley's California
novels portray an encounter with a unique region qua state
of mind--centered in Hollywood--possessing a rich mythical
and symbolic resonance. Into this vast carpet of dreams are
threaded the myths of the new world, the frontier, the old
west; the chance for new beginnings, freedom, and success;
and the thriving of the entrepreneurial spirit. Here also are
the cults of youth, beauty, leisure, sun, money--set against
a stunning landscape of ocean, mountains, and desert. But
all with an apocalyptic undertone, for this is a precarious
paradise, doomed by earthquakes, slides, decadence, its own
embarras de richesses. As such, California represented for
Huxley an especially fecund subject and setting for his ideas
about the perils of modern civilization, and how best to save
man from himself. Huxley in these two novels was reacting
to the mythological Hollywood so well described by Jonas Spatz
in his study Hollywood in Fiction: Some Versions of the American Myth:

> Hollywood, in its social, economic, political, artistic
> and moral atmosphere, is somehow a commentary on,
> or a microcosm of, contemporary Western civilization
> in general and American culture in particular. In
> a world precariously balanced between destruction
> and utopia, Hollywood seems to exhibit both the
> promise of modern civilization and the symptoms of
> the decline of the West. Its major product, the mo-
> tion picture, is both a revolutionary instrument for
> the entertainment and education of the masses and a
> dangerous weapon for their corruption and enslave-
> ment. Thus, Hollywood possesses a particular vital-
> ity to commentators of all political and social disposi-
> tions because it appears characteristic of the unique
> condition of modern man in an industrial society.[2]

Finally, there is an added complexity in that Huxley was viewing this California as a European; a California which is simultaneously a microcosm of America, the New World and like nothing else in America. The European in America--the more so in California--finds himself a stranger in a strange land. His vision of America, while highly refracted, may also demonstrate the clarity possessed only by an outsider. His status as an outsider is both his greatest liability and his greatest asset as a reporter, since he carries with him both his own preconceived notions of reality and a fresh eye for oddities about the local scene which the native takes for granted.

California Dreaming: "After Many a Summer Dies the Swan"

> The woods decay, the woods decay and fall,
> The vapours weep their burthen to the ground,
> Man comes and tills the field and lies beneath,
> And after many a summer dies the swan.
> Me only cruel immortality
> Consumes.
>
> --from Tennyson, Tithonus

Of the success stories which epitomize the myth of the American Dream, as well as its perils, none is more colorful than that of newspaper tycoon William Randolph Hearst, who, with his mistress Marion Davies, led a fantastic life in the '20s and '30s at his fabulous castle at San Simeon, California. While Hearst's story, as a study of wealth, power, eccentricities, and the loneliness these bring, forms the basis of Orson Welles' seminal film of 1941, Citizen Kane (which Hearst tried to suppress), it was Aldous Huxley who had first fictionalized Hearst's story in After Many a Summer Dies the Swan. And Welles knew of it. For in fact, at the end of July 1939, Aldous and Maria Huxley had celebrated Aldous' birthday and the completion of After Many a Summer by having a big luncheon party which was attended by the elite of Hollywood: Charles Chaplin, Paulette Goddard, Helen Hayes, Charles MacArthur, the Edwin Hubbles, Constance Collier, Christopher Wood, Gerald Heard, Lillian Gish--and, just arrived in Hollywood in July, under carte blanche contract to RKO, the boy

wonder Orson Welles.[3] At this point Welles had other projects in mind for his Mercury Players and had not yet hit
upon the idea of Hearst as a subject. Since it was not until
the spring of 1940 that Welles and Herman J. Mankiewicz wrote
the script of Citizen Kane (at first titled "American"), it is
quite possible that Welles' story of the rise and fall of Charles
Foster Kane, his relationship with Susan Alexander, and their
life at Xanadu was at least partly inspired by Huxley's treatment of Hearst in After Many a Summer.[4]

One of the things which especially interested Huxley in
Hearst was the tycoon's notorious fear of death, a fear made
all the more onerous when set against the youth culture of
California. Huxley here made use of a mythological prece-
dent for this quest for longevity. Tithonus of Tennyson's
poem, source of Huxley's title for this novel, had bad luck
when he tried to tamper with the natural order of things.
In the myth, Tithonus asked for immortality, which was
granted him through the intercession of his beloved Aurora,
Goddess of Dawn, by Zeus. But, forgetting to ask for eternal youth and vitality, Tithonus grew older and older yet
could not die; the sting of immortality was far worse than
that of death. This search for longevity through the out-
witting of time receives a bizarre rendition in Huxley's novel,
set in decadent southern California, land of eternal youth
and beauty. Tycoon Jo Stoyte, fearing death and desperately
seeking to prolong his life, is ultimately willing to submit himself to a diet of carp guts which has kept the Fifth Earl of
Gonister alive for two centuries. The Earl is still virile but
has reverted to a grotesque simian state, caged with his similarly preserved concubine in a cellar in England. The condition of these two, and that of their surroundings, evokes an
utter travesty of the opulent life at San Simeon.

It is strange work indeed. Despite a generally mixed
reaction to the novel, After Many a Summer (published in
England with the shorter title) won the University of Edin-
burgh's James Tait Black prize as the best novel of 1939.
One may wonder about other British novels of that year, and
might be surprised to learn of the quality of the competition:
Henry Green's Party Going, Anthony Powell's What's Become
of Waring, and Christopher Isherwood's Goodbye to Berlin--
not to mention James Joyce's Finnegans Wake. It was also a
banner year for the California novel: John Steinbeck's The
Grapes of Wrath, Raymond Chandler's The Big Sleep, and

Nathanael West's The Day of the Locust. The eve of war
brought out an extraordinary burst of creativity.

How did Huxley come to write such a novel, his first
to use Los Angeles and its peculiar culture as a springboard
for his philosophical ideas about the nature of reality and
how we ought to live? It was written as part of his immediate
reaction to his arrival in that very different world. As early
as October 1938, in the midst of Huxley's work on the treatment for Madame Curie, Maria wrote that Huxley was starting
a new novel: "This one is about longevity, and is going to
be comic too.... He is going to put in a lot about California
life...."[5] The following February Huxley himself described
the novel, which, in something like the manner of Brave New
World,

> is a phantasy, but built up of solidly realistic
> psychological elements; a wild extravaganza, but
> with the quality of a most serious parable.[6]

There was definitely to be a message in the medium. In Huxley's speaking of a "parable," we are reminded of the parable-
art of the 1930s, which W. H. Auden had defined as "that
art which shall teach man to unlearn hatred and learn love."[7]
The use of fiction-as-parable in the '30s has been examined
thoroughly in Samuel Hynes' The Auden Generation. Hynes
reaches this definition:

> a parable is functional--that is message-bearing,
> clarifying, instructive--but it is not didactic. Rather
> it is an escape from didacticism; like a myth, it
> renders the feeling of human issues, not an inter-
> pretation of them. It is non-realistic, because it
> takes its form from its content, and not from an
> idea of fidelity to the observed world. It is moral,
> not aesthetic, in its primary intention; it offers
> models of the problem of action. The working out
> of the meaning of parable, in theory and in para-
> bolic practice, is a process that continued through
> the 'thirties, and gave a kind of formal continuity
> to the diversity of 'thirties writing.[8]

Although sprinkled with what could be considered didacticism,
After Many a Summer at the same time resembles this description of parable-art.

But there is another way to approach Huxley's work, the work he had described upon finishing it in July 1939 as "a kind of fantasy, at once comic and cautionary, farcical, blood-curdling and reflective."[9] After Many a Summer, a combination of fantasy and morality, a mixture of modes and moods, is essentially a satire; specifically, as Northrop Frye would classify it, a Menippean satire.[10] Extroverted, intellectual, concerned with scrutinizing mental attitudes and ideas, the form was ideal for Huxley's purposes. As one of the key characters in the book, Mr. Propter, explicitly affirms,

> a good satire was much more deeply truthful and, of course, much more profitable than a good tragedy. The trouble was that so few good satires existed, because so few satirists were prepared to carry their criticism of human values far enough.[11]

Huxley was so prepared--to carry his satire to the extreme-- even though he risked the wrath of his readers, many of whom decided that art had been sacrificed to moral lesson, and charity to moral judgment. Typical of the negative responses to the novel is this one by Charles M. Holmes: "By glorying in the weaknesses of personalities he has created, Huxley exposes a lack of charity in his own."[12] But to take this tack is to misunderstand the very nature of satire, and of Huxley himself. Peter Bowering put the case very well:

> If we accuse Huxley of a lack of warmth, a lack of sympathy towards humanity, then we fail to discern the essential difference between the satirist and the objects of his satire. Huxley's style, his clinical detachment--at times as subtle and stark as that of that other master of irony, Swift himself--is in itself a manifestation of the attitude he is satirizing.[13]

Using the form of the Menippean satire, Huxley comes to grips with the fantastic culture of southern California and uses it as a way to deal with America's vulgarity and materialism--symptoms of a larger moral failure. We see these things in Huxley's satirization of Jo Stoyte's castle, modeled on that of William Randolph Hearst's at San Simeon, which the Huxleys had visited. And in Stoyte's Beverly Pantheon Cemetery--obviously Forest Lawn Memorial Park, which we know astonished and fascinated Huxley as much as it would

Evelyn Waugh, who parodied it in 1948 as "Whispering Glades"
in The Loved One. On that subject we note one of the advertisements for the cemetery as recalled in an essay by
Christopher Isherwood,

> in which a charming, well-groomed elderly lady (pre-
> sumably risen from the dead) assured the public:
> "It's better at Forest Lawn. I speak from exper-
> ience."[14]

And Isherwood paid a kind of tribute to his friend Huxley
when he made After Many a Summer Died the Swan part of
a classroom discussion by the college professor George in Isherwood's 1964 novel, A Single Man.

In his examination of what he found to be the amazing
environment of southern California, Huxley could probe the
divergent elements of life in America, and modern life in
general: the spiritual versus the material, the sacred versus
the profane, immortality--or survival--versus mortality. From
the beginning to the end of the novel, these polar elements
are constantly vying for the attention of the characters, as
well as of the reader. It is the intent of Huxley's novel to
show the way out of the wrenching caused by these dichoto-
mies which characterize the unregenerate world: the way of
mysticism, the transcendence of personality, the contemplative
life.

Thus, by means of satire we have the message of salvation through mysticism, reflecting Huxley's continuing interest in the way of life he had begun to explore earlier in Eyeless in Gaza and Ends and Means. Now, in Los Angeles, his
beliefs were fostered by his association with mystics like
Gerald Heard and Krishnamurti. The way of mysticism requires the surrendering of ego, of personality; the admission
of being nothing so that God, or divine something, can enter.
To try to escape ourselves through other means--such as
pleasure or possessions--only leads us deeper into the mor-
ass. We may seek escape through myriad means, as the narrator describes:

> In the frenzies of gambling and revivalism; in the
> monomanias of avarice and perversion, of research
> and sectarianism and ambition; in the compensatory
> lunacies of alcohol, of reading, of day-dreaming, of

> morphia; in the hallucinations of opium and the cin-
> ema and ritual; in the wild epilepsies of political
> enthusiasm and erotic pleasure; in the stupors of
> Veronal and exhaustion. [pp. 152-153]

A rhetorical tour de force which drenches the reader in a
turbulent sea of manias, this catalogue covers most of the
diversions that man has discovered. Yet none of them can
prove satisfactory ultimately, for, as the narrator warns us,
"the addiction to pleasure tends to aggravate the condition
it temporarily alleviates" (p. 153). Huxley shows us characters caught in exactly the webs of pleasurable escape he has
described, in an environment which is most conducive to their
spinning: Los Angeles, a treacherous lotus land.

The characters in After Many a Summer are, in keeping
with the satiric form, one-dimensional figures embodying various types of humors, often with significant names, and all--
except one, Mr. Propter--are enthralled by some form of materialism and distorted sexuality. These characters interact
mostly in Stoyte's castle, a setting which recalls Huxley's earlier "country-house," neo-Peacockian novels (Crome Yellow
and Those Barren Leaves especially), here relocated to California. Jo Stoyte (like the protagonist in Citizen Kane) is
a vulgar tycoon from humble beginnings who has made good.
He is the American success story, but lives in a castle more
out of a nightmare than a fairy tale. Despite his millions,
he is an unhappy old man because he carries with him insecurities born of his fear of poverty and death. Competing
for his attention--his very soul, in fact--are the two characters representing the opposites of spiritualism and materialism: his friend William Propter, who lives in a modest house
nearby, and his personal physician-in-residence, Dr. Sigmond
Obispo.

Mr. Propter (whose name suggests, appropriately,
"proper," "prompter," and "ergo propter hoc," and who seems
modeled after Huxley's friend Gerald Heard) is the novel's
voice of mysticism and morality, a kind of "saintly" figure
who is the natural successor to a Huxleyan type we have
met before--in particular, Dr. James Miller of Eyeless in
Gaza. Propter serves as the satiric norm with whose voice
the reader is to ally himself. He asks us to surrender the
ego, to believe in the universal, everlasting nature of things
and in the idea that actual good is outside time. Despite the

lofty nature of his ideas regarding the way of mysticism,
Propter is pragmatic enough to realize that these ideas would
work best in a small group of enlightened individuals, with
a kind of Jeffersonian democracy--the kind of community Huxley had in mind when he helped Gerald Heard found Trabuco
College in 1942 near Laguna Beach, California, and when he
created Pala in his last novel, Island (1962).

Apropos of Mr. Propter, however, his long discourses
on the nature of reality and of the contemplative life are
seldom as interesting as the derangements he is denouncing,
a fact pertaining to dramatic rhythm, which accounted for
much of the criticism which the book garnered. As Keith
May succinctly put it, "Mr. Propter talks too much in relation
to the rest of the novel and is barely involved in the action."[15]
True, yet an exuberant display of great erudition about a
theme is characteristic of Menippean satire. The point is that,
in any case, Mr. Propter's deeds match his words. For example, he helps the migrant workers in the community, build-
ing decent cabins for them with his own hands; he experiments with using solar energy--all of which lends credence
to what he is offering to Jo Stoyte, and everyone else: ways
to find meaning in life; peace and eternity spiritually. The
philosophy which Mr. Propter proposes, with a metaphysical
basis, thus differs from the normal "second stage satire"
awareness (as defined by Frye) which is brought about
through "common sense," since Propter represents "uncommon
sense." In this way, After Many a Summer (like Eyeless in
Gaza) presents a change in the kind of satire (rational, classical) found in Huxley's earlier work.

On the other hand there is Propter's opposite in every
way, Dr. Sigmund Obispo (whose first name alludes to Freud,
while his last name refers to the location of San Simeon near
San Luis Obispo, as well as suggesting pontifical irony in the
Spanish word "obispo," meaning "bishop"). Obispo is, in
effect, a sham hierarch of the holy institution of medicine.
The supreme egoist thus joins the line of other Huxleyan
frauds in power: the Reverend Bodiham in Crome Yellow,
Dennis Burlap in Point Counter Point, the Arch Community
Singer in Brave New World, the eunuch Arch-Vicar in Ape
and Essence. Dr. Obispo promises longevity and virility to
Stoyte through scientific, material means, ultimately leading
to the bizarre panacea of ingesting carp guts. An oily, Me-
phistophelian figure without scruples, Dr. Obispo is essentially

an immoralist, a high priest of the church of latter-day sexuality, who postulates "sensuality for its own sake," and
everything for his sake.

One of Dr. Obispo's victims besides Stoyte is the tycoon's "daughter-mistress, child-concubine," Virginia Maunci-
ple (whose name ironically juxtaposes the suggestion of "virgin" with that of "manciple," which has its root meaning as
"possession" or "slave"). This character was loosely based
on Hearst's mistress, Marion Davies; Huxley had originally
named her "Dowlas" but he could not use it since it was too
close to Davies, and to her real name, Douras. As he wrote
to his publisher,

> The name Dowlas, I am afraid, has got to be changed,
> owing to its fortuitous resemblance to that of a no-
> torious lady in this neighborhood. I think that
> Maunciple should prove a sufficiently euphonious and
> safe substitute.[16]

Virginia is a madonna-whore figure, a promiscuous Catholic
who prays to Our Lady and derives equal meaning from sex
and Mass. But she loses a kind of innocence she retained
even while having "yum-yum" with "Uncle Jo," once the odi-
ous Dr. Obispo had managed to seduce her and

> had scientifically engineered her escape into an erotic
> epilepsy more excruciatingly intense than anything
> she had known before or even imagined possible....
> [p. 153]

Now she begins to experience the kind of misery which addiction to pleasure brings about. This new habit also compro-
mises her unconsciously tenuous relationships with both Stoyte
and Our Lady. Her lack of awareness, and that of people
in general, in fact, is exactly what Mr. Propter--and Huxley
--are seeking to abolish. As a miserable and unenlightened
character, Virginia lacks the means with which to extricate
herself from her situation. With superficial religious understanding, she can only go so far as to draw the curtains over
the shrine of Our Lady ("brilliantly illuminated by an ingenious system of concealed electric bulbs") in her room during
Obispo's visits. But as Huxley teaches us, covering up some-
thing--a metaphor for spiritual blindness--is no solution to a
problem, and no way to live.

The trait of unconsciousness, or unawareness, is shared by all the characters in the novel, except for Propter and Obispo, who are quite sure in their radically different ways of the nature of reality and of salvation. Other characters include Obispo's lab assistant Pete Boone, a romantic who idealizes both the Spanish Civil War and sad, sexy Virginia, and who unwittingly ends up dead by the hand of the jealous Stoyte, who mistakes him for Obispo with Virginia (thus this shooting will give Obispo some blackmailing leverage). Also there is Jeremy Pordage, the English scholar hired by Stoyte to edit the "Hauberk papers" in the castle, in which he makes the discovery in the Fifth Earl of Gonister's diary that that gentleman is still alive after two centuries as a result of eating the miracle food of carp intestines--a discovery which Obispo soon turns to his own advantage. Pordage prefers life in books to "direct, unmediated experience," and likes to reflect back upon his bi-weekly pilgrimages to a prostitute in London, where he enjoyed "infinite squalor in a little room." Pordage, as a detached intellectual, represents the "philosophus gloriosus," a prime object of attack in Menippean satire, since evil and folly are seen as diseases of the intellect. This type is rampant in Huxley's novels (as with Philip Quarles in Point Counter Point, and Hugh Ledwidge in Eyeless in Gaza, to name but two). Pordage, like others in the book except Propter, is caught up in the throes of materialism and misguided sexuality, yet is perhaps the one most comfortable in his unawareness and complacency.

But Pordage has another function as a character: as a stranger in a strange land, he provides the perfect mouthpiece through which Huxley can describe and comment on what he finds in Los Angeles, by which means he can also comment on America (and modern life) in general. In this respect the satire of After Many a Summer takes a broader turn. From his first arrival in Los Angeles, Pordage is the sounding board for the competing elements of the spiritual and the material which he continuously encounters. The city itself, which he describes en route from the downtown train station to Hollywood, Beverly Hills, and Stoyte's castle in the San Fernando Valley, is wildly heterogeneous in every way: its inhabitants, neighborhoods, architectural styles--and its representations of ideologies. Besides viewing the various styles of fantastic commercial sights, churches, and homes--"like the pavilions at some endless international exhibition"--Pordage spots a series of telling signs.

These advertisements cogently exemplify the motifs of
the spiritual and material, the mortal and immortal, elements
which strive to gain our allegiance in Los Angeles, and in
modern life in general. Among them are:

> FINE LIQUORS.
> TURKEY SANDWICHES.
> GO TO CHURCH AND FEEL BETTER ALL THE WEEK.
> WHAT IS GOOD FOR BUSINESS IS GOOD FOR YOU.
> ....
> JESUS IS COMING SOON.
> YOU TOO CAN HAVE ABIDING YOUTH WITH THRILL-
> PHORM BRASSIERES.
> BEVERLY PANTHEON, THE CEMETERY THAT IS
> DIFFERENT. [p. 8]

Even in the mere listing of these advertisements, as amorphous
icons of decadent life, Huxley has set the groundwork for
his satire. A society which vulgarizes religion, along with
Pain, Sex and Time (the title of a 1939 treatise by Gerald
Heard dealing with similar concerns to Huxley's), and places
them on the same superficial level as eating, drinking, and making money, is a society in need of heightened self-awareness,
not selfishness; spiritual transformation, not transgression.
Only then would the words of Dr. Mulge, seeking an endow-
ment for his college from Stoyte, come true: that there is a

> "New Civilization that is coming to blossom here in
> the West.... The Athens of the twentieth century
> is on the point of emerging here, in the Los Angeles
> Metropolitan Area." [p. 57]

Pordage's description of Stoyte's "Beverly Pantheon,
The Personality Cemetery" further compounds the impression
of decadence in this hothouse world. Huxley himself took
delight in the original of this cemetery; in March 1939, while
in the midst of writing this novel, Huxley entertained a young
European visitor, Jeremy Hutchinson, whose recollection of
his visit includes the following:

> Within an hour of arriving ... I was being conducted
> round Forest Lawn with Aldous caressing the marble
> pink bottoms of the statuary and pointing out the
> "staggering sensuality" as the eternal Wurlitzer sounds
> came out from behind the trees....[17]

"Staggering sensuality" is a most incisive phrase to describe
the phenomenon. The name "Beverly Pantheon" was also
well chosen, suggesting not only a burial place but "all gods"
--including Mammon, Dionysus, and Eros.

Stoyte's monument valley is a "cemetery like an amusement park" (Pordage's apt simile), replete with the Perpetual
Wurlitzer and the Tower of Resurrection, reproductions of
churches and the Taj Mahal, numerous nubile nymphs as
statuary and Rodin's Le Baiser. It is all run by an adroit
manager who has initiated the idea of

> injecting sex appeal into death; he who had reso-
> lutely resisted every attempt to introduce into the
> cemetery any representation of grief or age, any
> symbol of mortality, any image of the sufferings of
> Jesus. [p. 156]

A sexy cemetery, sans souci? Sex appeal--the best way to
remove the sting from suffering and death? Mark Staithes
was wrong when he told Anthony Beavis in Eyeless in Gaza
that death was "the only thing we haven't succeeded in com-
pletely vulgarizing"[18] (but then Huxley had not yet seen
Forest Lawn). If Forest Lawn, alias the Beverly Pantheon,
represents the extreme version of the American way of vulgarizing life and death, it provides fertile ground for Huxley's advocacy of the need to recapture true spiritual values
and the proper perspective, as he came to understand those
things.

The motif of the confusion between the sacred and the
profane is continued with considerable amplification in Stoyte's
bizarre castle (the castle would be rendered in a similarly
Gothic fashion in Citizen Kane). Within this splendor striving to be baronial, this Xanadu of incongruity, are furnish-
ings which evince the confounding of its residents. Pordage
is amazed to find, among other things, the great hall where
at one end is hung El Greco's Crucifixion of St. Peter, at
the other a Rubens nude; Virginia's elegant Louis XV boudoir,
complete with a Watteau and a "fully equipped soda fountain
in a rococo embrasure"; a library with woodwork by Grinling
Gibbons, but no books; a smaller dining room with a Fra An-
gelico, and furniture from Brighton Pavilion; a Vermeer in
the elevator.

This turmoil of morality and taste is carried on externally as well. A high contrast is provided between the medieval pomp of the castle on the hill, complete with donjon, portcullis, and moat, and the poverty of the Okies working in the orange groves below. Immediately surrounding the castle are such wildly divergent adornments as a tennis court, a replica of the sacred grotto at Lourdes, a bronze nymph by Giambologna with water spouting from her breasts, and an enclosed group of baboons. This strange conglomeration, like the collection of advertisements discussed above, blatantly expresses the vulgarity and decadence of this world.

It also introduces a prime example of the simian references rampant in After Many a Summer. For example, Stoyte is thought of as a "barrel of hairy flesh" by Virginia, and she will later call Obispo a "lousy apeman" as he is about to seduce her. One of the most important references occurs about a quarter way through the book when Virginia observes two of the baboons copulating: "'Aren't they cute!' she cried. Aren't they human!'" (p. 64). This scene of human-like apes ironically prefigures the last scene in the book, in which Virginia, Stoyte, and Obispo have gone to a house in England seeking that long-preserved, virile Earl of Gonister. They discover him in the cellar with his mistress, all right--but in a cage. Here is the Earl amidst the stench, transfigured into a hairy ape, wearing only a filthy tattered shirt; even the skull has changed, with a protruding brow. His mate has also grown simian, but with "pendulous and withered dugs." When Stoyte asks, "What's happened to them?" Obispo airily replies, "Just time." In a few minutes, after some scuffling and yelping, then growling, old Earl and his girl are busily engaged in the same activity as the baboons had been. Even more shocking than finding these two humans reverted to a hairy, grotesque animal state is that, despite it all, Stoyte is so desperate, so degenerate, that he is still willing to go through with the plans to obtain longevity through ingesting carp intestines (the Earl is presently 201 years old). Stoyte wonders how long it would take to become like the Earl:

> "I mean, it wouldn't happen at once ... there'd be a long time while a person ... well, you know; while he wouldn't change any. And once you get over the first shock--well, they look like they were having a pretty good time. I mean in their own way, of course. Don't you think so, Obispo?" [p. 241]

The book ends with Obispo laughing.

But it is a macabre laugh; a wry comment, like the whole book in its own way, on the nature of man and beast. Yet, as Keith May has rightly affirmed, Huxley's point is that man differs from animals not in degree only, but rather in the "ability to be conscious of consciousness."[19] When man loses his spiritual consciousness he does descend to the level of the ape, as has the Earl of Gonister. In a less dramatic, but no less real way, so has Jo Stoyte. For Stoyte has rejected the way of the spirit as shown by Propter, and has elected to follow the way of the flesh, and of "science," as guided by Obispo. Stoyte may live, but it will be a living death. With After Many a Summer, Huxley was trying to wake up those who are presently the living dead, in a spiritual sense. That he set his "fantasy" and "parable" in the particular locale of Los Angeles--a place with mythical resonance--only increased the ramifications of his message. For Huxley, the way out of moral decay and its attendant social problems is the way of enlightenment, of mysticism, of increased awareness so that our best potentialities may be actualized. This would always be a concern of Huxley's; he said it another way in this 1939 letter:

> So long as the majority of human beings choose to live like the homme moyen sensuel, in an "unregenerate" state, society at large cannot do anything except stagger along from catastrophe to catastrophe.[20]

The Lost Screenplay: "Ape and Essence"

> But man, proud man,
> Drest in a little brief authority--
> Most ignorant of what he is most assur'd.
> His glassy essence--like an angry ape,
> Plays such fantastic tricks before high heaven
> As make the angels weep.
>
>   --Shakespeare, Measure for Measure

With Ape and Essence Huxley continued to try to stir

us into deeper awareness of ourselves and our society, by showing us what may happen if we continue on a thoughtless course, as "unconscious of consciousness" as apes. But the book is unique in Huxley's canon both in its format--that of a screenplay--and in the depth of the horror it portrays-- that of Los Angeles in the year 2108, after the nuclear holo- caust of World War III. The form of this novel can only be attributed to Huxley's experience as a screenwriter for ten years; its subject, to his despair over World War II and the implications of the atomic bomb.

Using the form of the screenplay with which he had be- come so well acquainted in Hollywood, Huxley found that he could present his parable in a more intense, multi-media kind of way--with words, music, visuals, and special effects. As Maria Huxley described the book when Aldous had finished it in February 1948,

> It is also in a very interesting medium. The scenario form giving room for very beautiful descriptions of nature, for music, for poetry. Excellent medium for cutting out all that he does not actually need and for getting in, via the narrator, all that he needs to say. [21]

But though the use of the screenplay form was well-suited to Huxley's intentions, it seems to have met with resistance in some readers, as we see in this letter from Huxley to author Philip Wylie in 1949:

> You are probably right in what you say about the form of Ape and Essence. And yet there was no other form that would do. I tried at first to write it "straight"; but the material simply wouldn't suffer itself to be expressed at length and in realistic, verisimilitudinous terms. The thing had to be short and fantastic, or else it could not be at all. So I chose the scenario form as that which best fulfilled the requirements. [22]

Far more than form, though, it was the content of Ape and Essence that provoked controversy. Huxley's intentions be- hind this "short and fantastic" material were misunderstood by many readers who could not see the message of salvation behind the grotesquery, as is shown in this comment by a

reviewer in 1949: Huxley "does not care enough what happens to mankind, or he would not describe their degradation
in that particular way."[23]

Of course that comment misses the point entirely. Huxley cared supremely about the fate of mankind, and made that
concern the focus of his fiction. The comment also fails to
take into account genre and context. Essentially a satiric
utopia, Ape and Essence describes the horrible degradation
of man not out of misanthropic glee, but as a warning to
man that if he keeps on as he is, blindly worshipping science
and technology, these can eventually enslave rather than lib-
erate him. As such Huxley presents a negative utopia akin
to that of Brave New World, but with this difference, as noted
by Peter Firchow:

> where he had earlier seen man doomed to blissful
> lunacy in the orgy-porgian embrace of science, he
> now saw him even more inevitably crushed by the
> cataclysmic collapse of that very same science.[24]

Huxley's scenario presents a vision of a terrible world,
full of hatred, violence, and deformity, but it is not exactly
like that of the third stage of satire as described by Northrop Frye[25] and exemplified in Swift's Gulliver's Travels or
West's The Day of the Locust, for Huxley offers us a second
stage norm of common sense, and a means to escape that terrible world. In Island (1962), his third and final utopian
novel, Huxley would present a positive utopia in the isle of
Pala, a place free, at least for a time, of the evils which
Huxley had been warning us about for so long: overpopulation, militarism, mechanization, worship of science,
coercive politics, destruction of the environment. These are
the very problems which are responsible for the horrible
world depicted in Ape and Essence.

Ape and Essence consists of two parts which reflect
upon one another: there is a very brief prose introduction
which sets the scene for the finding of the lost screenplay
"Ape and Essence," which forms the bulk of the novel. Both
sections also revolve upon the movie industry and its locale
--and the mythical qualities of each. The introductory section ("Tallis"), which begins in a movie studio, concerns the
conversation and differing interests of screenwriter Bob Briggs
and an unnamed first-person narrator, presumably a writer,

who represents Huxley's philosophical and moral views. The
section has clear references to certain events of 1947-48, both
in Huxley's personal life and in the world. It begins with
an extraordinary juxtaposition of Gandhi, Christ and man,
describing a day which is clearly January 30, 1948:

> It was the day of Gandhi's assassination; but on
> Calvary the sightseers were more interested in the
> contents of their picnic baskets than in the possible
> significance of the, after all, rather commonplace
> event they had turned out to witness. In spite of
> all the astronomers can say, Ptolemy was perfectly
> right: the center of the universe is here, not there.
> Gandhi might be dead; but across the desk in his of-
> fice, across the lunch table in the Studio Commissary,
> Bob Briggs was concerned to talk only about him-
> self. [26]

This Bob, as the narrator tells us, had troubles stem-
ming from his marriage and his mistress, but "he didn't really
want to be helped. He liked being in a mess and, still more,
he liked talking about his predicament" (p. 1). A discussion
develops, touching on Bob, "bound and committed to adultery
no less irrevocably than Gandhi had been bound and committed to nonviolence and prison and assassination" (p. 3).
For Huxley, Bob represents a typically complacent, non-aware
person, content to sit back and let his world go to hell; someone not concerned about the implications of the non-violent
Gandhi's death by violence. That was the sort of person
Huxley wanted to shock into awareness with Ape and Essence.

In this first section Huxley presents a dichotomy between Bob's superficial comments--whether on adultery,
Gandhi, or movies--and the narrator's interior, moral reactions. Thus he sets the meaning of Gandhi's life and death
against the thoughtlessness of the world. And we have discussed earlier how the narrator imagines paintings of "Christ
before Lublin" when Bob relates the story of his failure to
get a raise from the producer ("in this Studio, at this time,
not even Jesus Christ himself could get a raise"), an anecdote
derived from Huxley's experience in the making of the film
A Woman's Vengeance.

Another interesting example of how Huxley works his
personal experiences into his fiction is his use of the figure

St. Catherine of Siena, a fourteenth-century Italian ascetic
and mystic. Huxley, as can be seen in his letters as early
as 1946, had planned to write an historical novel about her;
he wondered about handling "religious matters in fictional
form."27 The novel did not materialize, but she now appears
in Ape and Essence as the subject of a film script, "Catherine
of Siena," on which Bob had worked. Bob talks about it as
a truck goes by bearing some of the props, such as the
Italianate cathedral door; it is to be the new picture of movie
star "Hedda Boddy." Bob describes the rewriting of his
script--a process which Huxley himself knew all too well--by
a team whose names parody the incongruous backgrounds of
writers in Los Angeles: "O'Toole-Menendez-Boguslavsky"
(italics mine). The subject of Catherine reminds the narrator
of Gandhi in some ways. Both were "saints in politics," he
tells Bob; she died too young, or they would have killed her
too--and he wonders if the script goes into that. Bob replies
no, that would be "Too depressing.... The public likes its
stars to be successful" (p. 9). Rather than talk about church
politics, which would be, says Bob, "anti-Catholic and might
easily become un-American" (a direct reference to the HUAC-
McCarthy trials beginning in 1947), the film plays it safe and
concentrates on the love interest, "the boy she dictated her
letters to." Huxley here demonstrates the movie industry's
(and modern society's) vulgarization of otherwise controversial
religious-political material. But this is nothing when compared
to what happens to religion and politics after the nuclear
holocaust depicted in the script which Bob and the narrator,
and we, shall read.

When a truck goes by on its way to the incinerator and
some rejected scripts fall off, the two writers discover a very
weird treatment, "Ape and Essence," written by "William Tallis,
Cottonwood Ranch, Murcia, California," and which includes,
here and there, strange poetry (such as "Ends are ape-chosen;
only the means are man's"). Reading the script, and curious
about its author, they decide to drive out to his desert home
to see him. The ranch is located just north of the San Gabriel
mountains above Los Angeles, a setting identical to Huxley's
own desert retreat at Llano. The occasion provides him with
the opportunity to describe the strange quality of light and
vegetation in the desert which he loved: the "soft rich grays
and silvers, the pale golds and russets" of the sagebrush,
bunch grass, and so on; the "strangely gesticulating" Joshua

trees; the "abrupt and jagged buttes"; the shifting light pro-
ducing an "incandescence" in the scene (pp. 12-13).

In this setting of stark natural beauty Bob and the
narrator discover Tallis' house, and the family now occupying
it who had earlier rented it to him. This family enacts a domestic situation which will provide a sharp contrast to the
situation found in the world of "Ape and Essence," while at
the same time demonstrating its roots. The old couple (who
resemble "Ma and Pa Kettle") tell the writers that Tallis has
been dead six weeks. Tallis had written the script to make
some money to send to his granddaughter in Europe. The
narrator wonders perhaps whether she wasn't one of those
destitute children in post-war Europe, referred to in Tallis'
script, who were prostituting themselves for a bar of choco-
late--another example of the atrocities of war and man. The
two grandchildren of the old couple, also living in Tallis'
house, have a deeper significance to the story than may at
first be thought. Rosie, about sixteen, wants to get into
the movies; wily Bob soon sees the amorous opportunities in
that situation and plies her with the line that he will see about
getting her a screen test. The other teenage granddaughter,
Katie, is already burdened with a baby; though the old couple
say she was "married" last year, the implication is otherwise.
As the writers leave the house, the narrator hears Katie in
the bathroom rinsing out diapers; he cautions Bob to "Listen!"
Bob says, "To what?"--whereupon the narrator shrugs, thinking, "Ears have they, neither do they hear" (p. 24). Though
satirically juxtaposed with a scatological incident, this urging
to "listen" is the same sort of warning as was shouted by the
mynas in Island: "Attention. Attention"--be aware. The
point of Huxley's describing Bob Briggs and the family now
living in Tallis' desert retreat is to show us people more concerned with pursuing the satisfaction of their own egos, am-
bitions, lusts, than with reaching a deeper awareness of the
human condition. The script which follows, repulsively depicting the future consequences of present-day sins of omis-
sion and commission, will try to shock us out of our complacency.

The script "Ape and Essence," with a narrator's commentary interspersed throughout, begins by establishing the
background for the nuclear holocaust. We need to pay close
attention to the first few pages especially, which set up just
what Huxley is up to. The first shot is described as being,

in "something better than Technicolor ... the hour before
sunrise," a view of "an almost unruffled sea." We hear music in the style of Debussy, free of all "Wagnerian lubricity
and bumptiousness" (and, he need not add, Hitlerian associ-
ations). The scene is an "emblem of an emblem of Eternity,"
while the script's voice-over provides a commentary on the
inefficacy of art (in this case, film; but Huxley had often
said the same about novels) to convey the full impact of nature, of reality. Yet, he goes on,

> Somehow you must be reminded
> Be induced to remember,
> Be implored to be willing to
> Understand what's What. [p. 26]

We fade out of this "emblem" and into the interior of a
"picture palace," crowded to the limit with well-dressed baboons, as the voice-over pronounces the relevant lines on
"ape" and "essence" from Shakespeare. The baboons are
watching a film in which a "bosomy young female baboon,"
all made up and wearing a "shell-pink evening gown," wad-
dles voluptously up to the "Louis XV microphone" on the
nightclub stage to sing. With her, on a leash and walking
on all fours, is Michael Faraday. In this shot and those following, where we see various "Folks in Radio Land, listening
in" (like a baboon housewife, baboon teenagers, a baboon
financier), where we see baboon armies, with Einsteins on
leash, engaged in nuclear and germ warfare, there is a crude
caricature, reminiscent of Swift, of the modern world where
men are depicted as baboons using science and technology to
destroy themselves. As George Woodcock aptly described this
satiric depiction,

> In After Many a Summer the baboons were the cap-
> tives of the cold, ruthless intellect of Dr. Obispo
> the scientist, but here it is the intellect that is cap-
> tive to the ape. [28]

Here, the apes force the collared Einsteins to pull the switches
releasing the nuclear missiles; as the narrator tells us, "Ape-
guided, those fingers, which have written equations and
played the music of Johann Sebastian Bach" (p. 35) now ini-
tiate the devastation of the earth. How did this come to be?
The narrator explains how fear--of science, technology, "Great
Men," war--lets us permit everything we don't want; how

(using a line from <u>A Woman's Vengeance</u>) "Love casts out
fear; but conversely fear casts out love," as well as intelligence, goodness, beauty and truth (p. 38). The credo is
now

> Church and State
> Greed and Hate:--
> Two Baboon-Persons in one Supreme Gorilla. [p. 34]

With a montage of shots depicting explosions, dead baboons, dying Einsteins, and the atomic mushroom cloud, "A
choking scream announces the death, by suicide, of twentieth-
century science" (p. 40). These shots of the actual nuclear
and bacterial war are inter-cut with shots of an exploring
party arriving much later to investigate the results of that
horrible debacle. It is now the year 2108, and some explorers
from New Zealand, spared the holocaust for reasons not hu-
manitarian but purely geographical, have come to rediscover
America from the West, now that the danger of radioactivity
has subsided after more than a century. Their ship lands
on the coast of southern California, near Los Angeles. One
of the exploring party, Alfred Poole, lingers behind the
group, and suddenly three raggedy, villainous-looking men
appear and drag him away into a gully. Then there is a dis-
solve to a panoramic view of southern California; as the camera plummets downward, we hear this voice-over presenting a
marvelous miscellanea:

> The sea and its clouds, the mountains glaucous-golden,
> The valleys full of indigo darkness,
> The drought of lion-colored plains,
> The rivers of pebbles and white sand.
> And in the midst of them the City of the Angels.
> Half a million houses,
> Five thousand miles of streets,
> Fifteen hundred thousand motor vehicles,
> And more rubber goods than Akron,
> More celluloid than the Soviets,
> More Nylons than New Rochelle,
> More brassieres than Buffalo,
> More deodorants than Denver,
> More oranges than anywhere,
> With bigger and better girls--
> The great Metrollopis of the West. [p. 46]

Jacob Zeitlin, Anna May Wong, and Aldous Huxley, Paramount
Studios, 1937

Aldous Huxley, West Hollywood, 1950

Aldous and Maria Huxley, Sienna, 1948

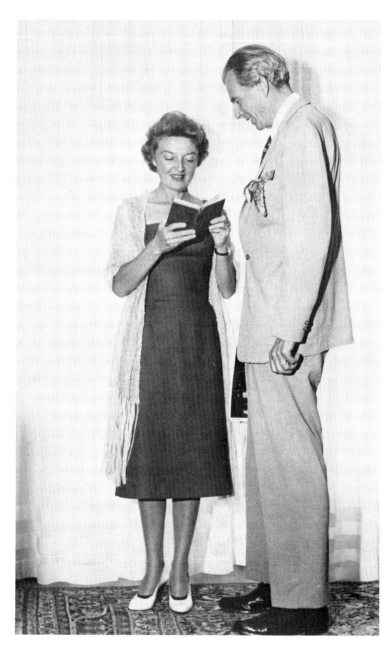

Aldous and Laura Huxley, Italy, 1958

Aldous Huxley, about 1960

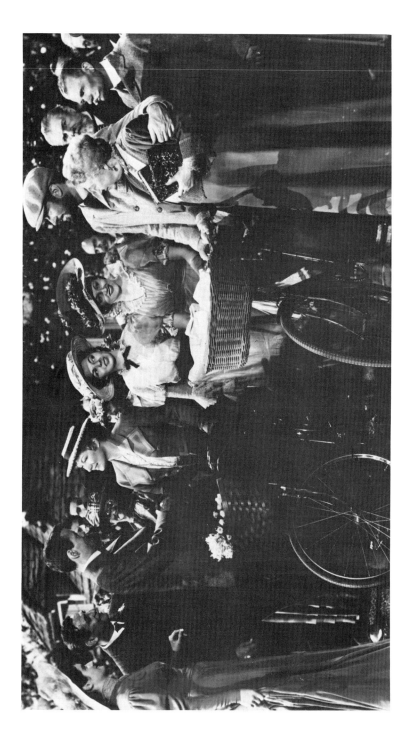

Walter Pidgeon and Greer Garson in Madame Curie (MGM, 1943)

Opposite: Robert Walker, Greer Garson, and Walter Pidgeon, Dame May Whitty in Madame Curie (MGM, 1943)

Laurence Olivier and Greer Garson in <u>Pride and Prejudice</u> (MGM, 1940)

Frieda Inescort, Laurence Olivier, Edward Ashley, Greer
Garson in Pride and Prejudice (MGM, 1940)

Maureen O'Sullivan, Greer Garson, Marsha Hunt, Heather
Angel, Ann Rutherford, Mary Boland in Pride and Prejudice
(MGM, 1940)

Peggy Ann Garner and Henry Daniell in <u>Jane Eyre</u> (20th Century-Fox, 1944)

Joan Fontaine and Orson Welles in Jane Eyre (20th Century-Fox, 1944)

Charles Boyer, Ann Blyth, and Jessica Tandy in A Woman's
Vengeance (Universal-International, 1947)

Jessica Tandy and Sir Cedric Hardwicke in A Woman's Vengeance (Universal-International, 1947)

Walter Pidgeon and Greer Garson in <u>Madame Curie</u> (MGM, 1943)

Hillary Brooke and Orson Welles in Jane Eyre (20th Century-Fox, 1944)

This satiric catalog mimicking Chamber of Commerce-Madison
Avenue lingo provides an ironic comment on what the screenplay suggests is on the screen--for as the camera gets closer
we see that Babylon has fallen. Los Angeles is now a ghost
town; "what was once the world's largest oasis is now its
greatest agglomeration of ruins in a wasteland" (p. 46). Appropriately, we land in Hollywood Cemetery. The tracking
camera reveals various mortuary monuments, including the
"more than life-size statue of Hedda Boddy ... 'Public Sweet-
heart Number One'" (p. 47)--a nice commentary on ars longa,
vita brevis.

     Suddenly, we meet a small group of people. Now, this
group, in the activity they are engaged in, in the way they
behave, in the way they are dressed, represents a microcosm
of the kind of society they are living in, here amidst the
desolation, just as the graveyard itself symbolizes the moral
and physical decay of humanity. For these people are gravediggers, searching for the clothing and jewelry no longer
available in their society, since there is no longer the knowledge or means with which to manufacture those kind of things.
The science and technology which enabled the nuclear world
war to occur have also destroyed that which had aided man.
Here, there are no more furnaces or turbines or factories.
There are no new buildings; the remnant of people must live
among the ruins of buildings, mostly those in the downtown
Los Angeles area, around Pershing Square, such as the old
Biltmore Hotel, or nearby at the remains of the University of
Southern California. And if the ruling elite want nice things,
they send their gravediggers out. So the Chief can now give
up the clothes once belonging to the "Production Manager of
Western-Shakespeare Pictures Incorporated" and slip into
something more conservative, the suit of the "Managing Director of the Golden Rule Brewing Corporation."

     The idea of the ruling elite brings us to the second
point about these people, their behavior, for they are essentially slaves in a society ruled by violence. They are kept
in line not by conditioning (as in Brave New World, where
"All conditioning aims at ... making people like their unes-
capable social destiny"),[29] but by fear. This is demonstrated
when one of the gravediggers is spotted secretly keeping for
himself a diamond ring he has found on a corpse. The
Chief lashes him with a whip. The worker will receive more
punishment this evening, since, as the Chief reminds him,
the gravedigger has robbed the State:

> "This is a Democracy.... We're all equal before the
> law. And the Law says that everything belongs to
> the Proletariat--in other words, it all goes to the
> State." [p. 49]

What a nice twisting of democracy and communism.

Also perverted in this society are ideas about sexuality,
marriage, women, and motherhood, all subsumed in a fantastic
perversion of religion. The immediate indication of all this
is found (and this brings us to the third aspect) in the way
these people are dressed. What is striking about their ap-
parel is not the identical, homespun shirts and trousers, but
what is worn over the strategic places: scarlet aprons em-
broidered with the word "NO." In addition, the women wear
"NO's" over each breast and on their seat: "Three unequiv-
ocal negatives greet us as they approach, two more, by way
of Parthian shots, as they recede" (p. 47). For this is a
society where sex is prohibited except for two weeks each
year during Belial festival; those who have not mutated sufficiently to conform to this rule are labeled "Hots" and are
punished. This prohibition on sex is a sign of the supreme
control of the rulers, themselves eunuchs, and is also a perversion of the Pope's dictum on celibacy. This society's
standards thus differ considerably from the codes of sexuality
established in Brave New World (with its standard of promiscuity, and the dispension of "Malthusian Belts" for contracep-
tion), and in Island (with its responsible free love, and the
teaching of the ecstasy of maithuna--the yoga of love).

In fact it seems that exploration of the idea of sexuality,
normal and otherwise (a favorite subject in satire) is part of
what stimulated Huxley to write Ape and Essence in the first
place, as we see in this letter of March 1947 to Anita Loos,
where he is talking about writing something on the future;
about, among other things,

> a post-atomic-war society in which the chief effect
> of the gamma radiations had been to produce a race
> of men and women who don't make love all the year
> round, but have a brief mating season. The effect
> of this on politics, religion, ethics etc. would be
> something very interesting and amusing to work out. [30]

The effect of all this was something more than interesting,

for in this society the gamma radiations produced not only
abnormal sexual behavior but disease and deformity amidst
the general devastation. The effects of the nuclear holo-
caust--called "The Thing" by its descendants--were not
understood scientifically, but explained by superstition. A
primitive religion evolved among the people, who could not
account for the atrocity of The Thing except that it must
have been caused by Belial. The rulers who enforce this
thought are a sham hierarchy of eunuch priests, led by "His
Eminence the Arch-Vicar of Belial, Lord of the Earth, Primate
of California, Servant of the Proletariat, Bishop of Hollywood"
(p. 77). They teach that Belial (more powerful than God)
works his evil through women, since it is women who produce
the horribly deformed offspring; hence the Catechism teaches,
"What is the nature of woman? Answer: Woman is the vessel
of the Unholy Spirit, the source of all deformity, the enemy
of the race...." (p. 55). Mating is therefore limited, marriage non-existent, and motherhood obscene. Mothers of deformed babies (those with more than the allowance of up to
three pairs of nipples, or seven toes or fingers) are punished,
their babies slaughtered en masse by impalement on a knife in
the horrible ritual on Belial Day, the Purification of the Race
--recalling the terror of the Biblical Slaughter of the Inno-
cents, as well as that of Hitler's insane purging of the Jews.
This bloody ritual, a gruesome parody of the Judeo-Christian
idea of sacrifice, is performed at the Los Angeles Coliseum
before a cheering congregation chanting "Glory to Belial, to
Belial in the lowest." The crowd is whipped into a spirit of
frenzy which precipitates an orgy, the beginning of two weeks
of indiscriminate mating. To read about this depraved society
which thrives in its own warped way on violence, ignorance,
misogyny, and misology is a ghastly experience, especially
when one realizes that Huxley is exaggerating ideas or tendencies that can be found in our own culture. One could not
stand to read about it, were it not relieved by some breath
of fresh air, some representation of normalcy and decency--
and some humor.

In this God-forsaken, Belial-obsessed desert, normality
with its comedy is provided by the timid New Zealand explorer
Alfred Poole--the kidnapped Dr. Poole--representative of the
Other World. It is through Poole's eyes that we view the
terrors of this society, and only because Poole manages to
keep himself alive through some quick thinking. We need to
back-track a bit here: when the Chief finds out that Poole

has come from a place where they still have trains (i.e., engines), he becomes very excited, believing that Poole could
help them "get it all going again. Like in the good old
days.... We'll have trains, real trains" (p. 53). This scene
is very similar to one in a movie Huxley had seen in London
in 1936, Things to Come, based on an H. G. Wells tract
about the holocaustal future of Europe.[31] This film, which
makes the point in the beginning that "if we don't end war,
war will end us," depicts the holocaust of war, famine, and
pestilence, decade by decade or so into the future. One scene
showing the broken-down society, where there is no more pe-
trol and flying is over, has a visitor from beyond landing in
a plane, coming to see how the survivors are doing. The
childish, stupid Chief (Ralph Richardson) tries to bully the
visitor (Raymond Massey) into providing him with the technical knowledge to get the old planes flying and "get things
moving again!" There are other similarities between this
film's futuristic society and that in Huxley's, such as the way
the film shows how thinking and reading are not encouraged:
"Who wants books to muddle our ideas?" the Chief exclaims;
people are to be trained "not to think, but to do." The same
thing is true in the horrible world of Ape and Essence: people (except the priests) cannot read, for knowledge is a dan-
gerous thing. Books from the Public Library are used for
fuel with which to bake bread. As the Chief remarks, "In
goes The Phenomenology of Spirit, out comes the corn bread.
And damned good bread it is" (p. 67).

But Poole first proves to be a disappointment to the
Chief when he explains that he knows nothing about engines.
He can't "get it all going again"--he is a botanist. The Chief
orders him buried alive; the others are delighted at the
prospect--"Goody goody!" Poole is saved only when it occurs
to him to use some psychology: as a botanist, he could be
useful, could help them get more to eat. The Chief relents;
Poole is dug out of his grave. The two women gravediggers
represent two diverging types in this society: there is the
mindlessly gleeful Flossie--"I hope you're not cross with me
because I wanted to bury you?... People look so screamingly
funny when they're being buried" (p. 58); then there is the
more sensitive Loola (who doesn't find these burials funny)--
secretly a "Hot," she will play a key role with Poole.

The character of Poole here functions on two levels:
first, this man is an outsider, a norm against which the

deviations of this society can be held. But Poole, who is a
"saint" when measured against the atrocious characters by
whom he finds himself held captive, falls far short of the
ideal when measured against other, Huxleyan standards. He
is a character who will undergo a kind of conversion or regeneration as a result of his experiences in broken-down
California. That is, Poole was a shy, mother-dominated, detached scientist. His extreme reverence for his mother (which
has so far prevented him from marrying, or, apparently, even
engaging in sex) provides an ironic contrast to this society's
profound scorn for women and contempt for motherhood (which
also represents a perversion of the Catholic reverence of
Mary, as Mother of God). At the same time, this extreme
attachment to his mother represents something unhealthy in
Poole which he will come to shed in his developing relationship with Loola, who is a throwback to previous humanity in
her capacity for kindness and for love. Poole and Loola soon
will learn the meaning of love from each other: Poole, who
was afraid to permit himself the experience of loving a woman
besides his mother, and Loola, whose society would not allow
the idea of love. Both develop their fuller humanity through
learning to care for one another.

Although their relationship will grow into something
far beyond the usual in this desolate society, it has its beginnings in part of that society's rituals. The consummation
of their relationship is graphically initiated at the orgy following the Purification Ceremonies, when Loola urges Poole to
yank away her "NO" patches, those signifiers of the Seventh
Commandment, those badges of "his mother's influence and all
his inhibitions, all the conventions in which he has been
brought up" (p. 109). After two weeks of concupiscent bliss
they are both converts to love, but now must carry on their
relationship surreptitiously, as love and commitment are not
permitted in this society. Because they are truly in love,
and awakened to the higher possibilities of life, they cannot
survive in the bleak society of 22nd-century California which
is predicated on all that is most base in man: hatred, greed,
violence, ignorance. In the final sequence of the script the
lovers escape Los Angeles and make their way north towards
Fresno, where "Hots" are acceptable, where they are "very
friendly to runaways from Southern California." The timid
Poole has developed courage and self-knowledge, and Loola
has progressed in her spiritual transformation under the tute-
lage of Poole, as seen in her reply, "Thank Bel ... I mean,

thank God" (p. 151). The characters--a potential Adam and
Eve--represent for Huxley's purposes the possibilities for a
new way of life, based on deeper self-awareness which would
in turn lead to a better society.

There is poetic--or film-script--justice on the final page
of "Ape and Essence," where the lovers, on their way through
the desert, find the tombstone of none other than "William
Tallis, 1882-1948." What appears, in "Twilight Zone" fashion,
to be a memento mori, Huxley has transformed into a sign of
regeneration. For inscribed on Tallis' tombstone are a few
lines from Shelley. It is a poem which Poole can complete
by reading its last lines in a book which he has with him:
"'The fire for which all thirst, now beams on me/Consuming
the last clouds of cold mortality'" (p. 152). A kind of death
leads to a kind of spiritual rebirth, a reawakening. The message of Ape and Essence is but one expression of that theme
which preoccupied Huxley in his later work; we must pay attention to eternity, not time--that is what will help save us
from ourselves. Huxley had said it this way--foreshadowing
Ape and Essence--in his novel of 1944, Time Must Have a
Stop:

> The divine Ground is a timeless reality. Seek it
> first, and all the rest--everything from an adequate
> interpretation of life to a release from compulsory
> self-destruction--will be added. Or, transposing
> the theme out of the evangelical into a Shakespearean
> key, you can say: "Cease being ignorant of what
> you are most assured, your glassy essence, and
> you will cease to be an angry ape, playing such
> fantastic tricks before high heaven as make the
> angels weep."[32]

CONCLUSION: SLOW FADE-OUT

In the years following Ape and Essence and A Woman's Vengeance, Huxley continued his interest in film projects, including those of a documentary nature, but he had less success in seeing them produced. Perhaps it was the nature of his writing; ironically, by the time he had rejected aesthetics for enlightenment as a primary focus, his craftsmanship--his regard for writing as an art--still set him apart from the Philistines. Perhaps he was just not working with the right people at the right time; in fact, in many of his ideas for films, he was ahead of his time. Another important reason is found in the changing times. Hollywood was coming out of its Golden Age, and it was no longer as easy for "serious" writers such as Huxley (or others, for that matter) to find work in the studios, for the studio system was beginning its slow decline in the late 1940s. The industry's peak year was 1946, when each week ninety million Americans (nearly 75% of the population) went to the movies; by 1955, the figure would shrink to forty-six million.[1] By the mid-1950s it was also clear that this was to be the era not of the moguls (most of them gone anyway) but of the independents.

Factors precipitating Hollywood's decline were many: the House Committee on Un-American Activities (HUAC) investigation, starting in 1947, of "Communism" in Hollywood, resulting in blacklisting, fear and cautiousness; the studios' loss of monopolistic control over film distribution in theatres (the "Consent Decree"); the reduction of the foreign market for American films; and the decreasing attendance at movies as a result of the increasing popularity of television. Hollywood would never be the same.

The halcyon days of the late '30s and early '40s, when the Huxleys enjoyed walks and picnics with their friends in the film industry, such as Anita Loos, Garbo, the Chaplins,

103

were also passing. Loos and Garbo moved to New York;
Chaplin was divorced from Paulette Goddard. In fact Chaplin in the 1940s incurred disfavor with the public which once
revered him: his private life was considered scandalous, and
his films, increasingly critical of social conditions, stirred
Right-Wingers to accuse him of Communist sympathies. Conditions eventually led to his exile in 1952 to Switzerland.
Huxley regarded Chaplin with sympathy, although he was
somewhat critical of his later film work.

In one of the few examples of Huxley's "film criticism"
we find this observation on Chaplin's Monsieur Verdoux (1947),
a black comedy which in its indictment of capitalism proved to
be his most controversial, least financially successful film:

> We saw "Monsieur Verdoux" the other day. What
> an aesthetic mess! He passes from a mime about
> murder which depends on not being taken seriously,
> to attempts at serious psychology which are supposed
> to be taken seriously & consequently make the murder-
> farce seem intolerable--because after all murder once
> removed from the world of childish make-believe, is
> not conceivably a subject for comedy. One feels
> terribly sorry for Charlie--such talents, such a
> mess--in art no less than in life. And all because
> he refuses to take anyone's advice about anything,
> but believing that, like the Pope he is infallible.[2]

Surprisingly, the arch-conservative Evelyn Waugh saw
Chaplin for what he was--an indomitable individualist. Waugh
had seen "a highly secret first performance of Charlie Chaplin's brilliant new film" while visiting in Los Angeles for six
weeks starting in February 1947.[3] For Waugh this was a time
of unsuccessful negotiations with M-G-M over a film version
of Brideshead Revisited, but also a time which we know provided him, through his fascination with Forest Lawn Memorial
Park, with inspiration for his satiric rendition of the American
way of life and death in The Loved One, a novel meant to top
Huxley's glancing blow at Forest Lawn in After Many a Summer. In a biting newspaper article on "Why Hollywood Is a
Term of Disparagement," Waugh praised Chaplin:

> Mr. Charles Chaplin, abused everywhere as a "pro-
> gressive," is the one genuine conservative artistically,
> in Hollywood. The others allow themselves no time
> to get at ease with their materials.[4]

Huxley still kept in touch not only with Chaplin but with Paulette Goddard. In April 1948 a new film project came up with Burgess Meredith, Paulette's husband, who wanted to make a scientific film on hypnotism, with Huxley to write the story. They and Anita Loos came to a luncheon to discuss the project at the Huxleys' in Wrightwood, where they saw demonstrations "by a man who uses hynotism to short-cut psychoanalysis and deals very successfully with sleep."[5] This was a subject which appealed to Huxley. Yet no more came of this idea than had the earlier plans of Meredith and Huxley to film Brave New World.

The big event of 1948, besides the publication in August of his anti-utopia set in California, Ape and Essence, was a film project which had Huxley back in Europe for three months, for the first time in eleven years. This project, proposed by director Zoltan Korda, financed by Alexander Korda, and to star Michèle Morgan, was to do an adaptation of Huxley's short story, "The Rest Cure."[6] The story (from his 1930 collection, Brief Candles) was based on an anecdote about a woman living opposite a friend of the Huxleys, Costanza Fasola, in Italy. To give the story a "post-war" setting, Huxley was to leave for Italy in June and write it there, the Korda organization paying him for story rights by financing the trip out of blocked currencies. It was a good trip: to Cherbourg, Paris, Siena, then Rome--staying at the Hôtel de la Ville above the Spanish Steps, dining in the Trattoria of the Via del Boccaccio frequented by cinema people like Roberto Rossellini and Anna Magnani (working at that time on the film L'Amore); then to Sanary, Paris, London. The Huxleys were able to see friends and relatives, and the trip made them realize how much they loved Europe, how much of a contrast was California. By September Huxley, finished with the film work, was hopeful of another successful venture like A Woman's Vengeance with Korda. But the film was not to be.

It was a rather slow year for Huxley in 1949, with no film work or books produced. Wintering at Palm Desert for health reasons, he had finished by February a stage version of Ape and Essence (which was never produced). He seems to have enjoyed a good social life and discussions about film, however. For example, he writes in March of dining with Constance Collier and Alfred Hitchcock, and learning more about the director's methods of film making:

[He] was very interesting about his new techniques
of movie making. He now shoots continuously a
whole reel at a time, doing everything without cutting, getting the necessary close-ups and inserts
and changes of distance by camera movements and
movements of the actors. The proceeding requires
long rehearsal and a team of technicians trained to
concert pitch. But apparently the results are remarkable.[7]

This letter provides some evidence of Huxley's interest in the
technical aspects of film making, though it seems he had not
yet seen the films Hitchcock was discussing. The director
had experimented with the technique of the continuous shot
in Rope (1948), with a somewhat contrived but interesting
effect as the result; he used a similar fluid camera style,
though to a lesser extent, in Under Capricorn (1949).

The summer of 1949 brought a renewal of Huxley's
friendship with Igor Stravinsky. They had met years before
in London, in 1928, through their mutual friend Victoria
Ocampo. Stravinsky reports they "saw a film together on
that occasion, Tolstoy's Resurrection" (the 1927 silent film
directed by Edwin Carewe, starring Dolores Del Rio).[8] Now
in California the Huxleys and the Stravinskys saw each other
often, going to plays, concerts, film previews together, or
meeting at their homes. Huxley in the summer had moved to
a large house in Los Angeles at 740 N. Kings Road, a block
north of Melrose Avenue. For Huxley, who liked to walk,
this was a good location, near La Cienega Boulevard, with
its fine shops, restaurants, and bookstores--including that of
Jacob Zeitlin, the bookseller and agent who had originally
sparked Huxley's interest in film work back in 1937. The
house was also not far from one of Huxley's favorite spots,
the Farmer's Market at Fairfax and Third. A diary entry on
August 10, 1949 by Stravinsky's friend Robert Craft illustrates
a typical day in the life of these emigrés in Los Angeles:

Lunch at the Farmer's Market with Christopher Isherwood and the Huxleys, the latter cooing at each other
today like newlyweds, or oldlyweds after a domestic
spat. Owing to its extensive variety of salads, seeds,
nuts, health foods, exotic fruit (Milton: "The sa-
voury pulp they chew, and in the rind"), the res-
taurant is a Huxleyan haunt. The other tables are

> held down by drugstore cowboys, movie stars, Cen-
> tral European refugees, and--judging from awed
> glances in our direction--Aldine and Igorian dis-
> ciples. All, for the nonce, are vegetarians, and all
> nibble at their greens like pasturing cows.[9]

The next few years brought very little film work for
Huxley; he supplemented his income by writing articles for
Esquire magazine. In the spring of 1950, Huxley and Isherwood again collaborated on an original screenplay eventually
called Below the Equator, apparently about revolutionary
violence in South America, but it never sold. Huxley's stage
play The Gioconda Smile was not a huge hit in New York.
One success of that year (although Huxley did not write the
screenplay) was the production in Britain of the film Prelude
to Fame (directed by Fergus McDonnell), based on Huxley's
short story about a child prodigy conductor, "Young Archi-
medes." In 1951 Huxley occupied himself with his study of
demon possession in The Devils of Loudon (published the next
year; it would eventually be filmed as The Devils by Ken Russell in 1971). Writing about their financial status, Maria said
Aldous could earn extra money from lectures and articles, but

> not movies obviously as he has been trying in vain
> to get a job since we are back and nothing turns
> up--Anita tried.... Now they are dithering about
> some readings with Ethel Barrymore....[10]

Finally, in December 1951 an interesting project developed with producer Gabriel Pascal, known for his films of
George Bernard Shaw's plays (Pygmalion, Major Barbara,
Caesar and Cleopatra). The idea was a film on Gandhi, with
the possibility of Huxley writing it and perhaps going to India in the autumn for the shooting. Huxley was enthusiastic
about the subject, for personal reasons. He had seen Gandhi
in India, while on the world tour Huxley had taken in 1925
and written about in Jesting Pilate. As we have seen, he had
also made discussion of Gandhi--assassinated in 1948 while
Huxley was finishing the book--an integral part of the beginning section of Ape and Essence, showing the contrast between events of world-wide significance and those of a purely
personal or trivial nature, which concern us more. The narrator here makes a point about Gandhi, who believed only in
people but got involved with nationalism, which was his un-
doing:

> It is not at the center, not from within the organ-
> ization, that the saint can cure our regimented in-
> sanity; it is only from without, at the periphery.[11]

This "saint" is a type we have met before in Huxley's fiction
(such as Dr. James Miller in Eyeless in Gaza, William Propter
in After Many a Summer). With Huxley's strong interest in
pacifism, Gandhi would have been an ideal subject for him to
treat in a screenplay.

But by May 1952 Huxley was beginning to have his
doubts about Pascal's ability to follow through; they had been
haggling since February:

> There is something simpatico about Pascal--he is a
> kind of Central European Baron Munchausen, boast-
> ful in an altogether childish way, mildly paranoiac,
> but well-meaning and honest, I believe, with those
> he likes, and when he can afford it. But he has
> the Bohemian's horror of being pinned down in black
> and white, of having to commit himself definitely to
> anything. Hence the difficulty of writing a satisfac-
> tory contract--particularly one which calls for con-
> ditional payments out of future earnings.[12]

As it turned out, that film was never made; again, it was a
matter of timing. Gandhi's story would not be filmed until
Sir Richard Attenborough's Gandhi of 1982, an Academy Award
winner.

The next year brought film ideas of differing kinds,
ranging from outer to inner space. First, from December
1952 to January 1953 Huxley was working on a project for
Frank Capra, a one-hour script for a popular science film on
the sun, which, as Huxley wrote,

> requires a great deal of reading (one must read
> 100% in order to be able to leave out 99%, as has
> to be done in this medium and for a TV audience)
> as well as a great deal of thought in regard to the
> ways in which information may be conveyed in terms
> of photographic and animated-cartoon images.[13]

What was Huxley knocking himself out for? The real story
behind Huxley's involvement in this project is revealed in

Frank Capra's autobiography, The Name Above the Title.   In
late 1952 Capra was approached by A.T.&T. about a new
television program on science which the Bell Telephone System was contemplating.   Capra advised them to make a pilot
film on the sun and he commissioned two experts each to write
a treatment: Willy Ley, scientist-writer, and Aldous Huxley,
"a writer who was Aristotle, Aquinas, Newton, Buddha, and
P. T. Barnum all mixed up into one incredible character,"
in Capra's words.   Though both treatments were excellent,
Capra also submitted his own "theatrical" version, based primarily on his research of Harvard astronomer Dr. Donald
Menzel's book, Our Mr. Sun.   Capra's version was

> in play form, all in dialogue, with two principal live
> characters, Dr. Research and a Fiction Writer, and
> four principal animated cartoon characters, Mr. Sun,
> Father Time, Thermo the Magician, and Chloro
> Phyll.[14]

Capra's "showman's" version was chosen over Ley's and Huxley's; on November 19, 1956, Our Mr. Sun was televised in
color nationally on CBS.

A major event of 1953 for Huxley was his beginning experimentation, under the supervision of Dr. Humphry Osmond,
with mescaline--for the purpose of probing and expanding the
consciousness.   This interest led to later experimentation with
LSD, and to Huxley's Blakean-inspired studies of psychedelic
drug use in The Doors of Perception (1954) and Heaven and
Hell (1956).   Perhaps these drug experiences heightened his
ability to visualize and increased his appreciation of pure
forms--and "pure cinema."   At any rate we do find him fascinated, for instance, with Francis Thompson's impressionistic,
semi-abstract study, N.Y., N.Y. (1954), a film using distorted
lenses and other methods which call attention to the medium
more than the subject.   Huxley discussed this film and its
genre in Heaven and Hell: it "does much more than merely
record and preserve the raw materials of non-representational
art; it actually turns out the finished product."[15]   The topic
was prefigured in a December 5, 1954 letter to Matthew which
touches on questions of spatial and temporal perception evoked
by Thompson's film:

> One would like to find out, first of all, why, as a
> matter of historical fact, so many cubists and other

abstractionists used forms which are identical with
those obtained by photographing reflections in
curved surfaces. Did the suggestion actually come
from hub caps and the backs of spoons? Or is there
a tendency in certain minds to perform the imaginative equivalent of projection on a curved surface?
Then there is the question of duration, of change
in time. Can a merely static art of distortion ever
convey anything like the rich significance of a dy-
namic art in time? The question, oddly enough,
hardly arises in relation to representational art.[16]

In addition to taking up such provocative questions as these
about the nature of art and film, in Heaven and Hell Huxley
also discussed the visionary quality of certain color documentaries, such as Disney's The Living Desert, where, at the
end, for example, the viewer finds himself sinking into the
cactus blossoms, "come straight from the Other World."[17]

The later years brought a few more film prospects. In
the fall of 1956 came the opportunity to do a film on the population problem--one of Huxley's causes--with director Fred
Zinnemann, who had done documentaries early in his career,
in addition to films such as High Noon, From Here to Eternity,
and Oklahoma!. They hoped that the Ford Foundation would
finance the project for its "Omnibus" television program.
There was an irony here which must not have been lost on
Huxley; it was Ford, a big industry in England in 1932,
which Huxley had satirized as the god of Brave New World
("Ford's in his flivver.... All's well with the world"). And
that was a world of enforced consumption, promiscuity, and
caste; in particular, of very strictly controlled population.
Now, in 1956, would the real Ford finance a film on the crisis
of overpopulation? Huxley wrote a synopsis on the subject,
and a later one in 1957 on overpopulation in Egypt. It was
an issue which he cared about deeply:

Whether anyone will put up the money, I don't know.
Everyone agrees that the population problem is the
most important problem of the present century; but
nobody wants to get in trouble with the Papists.[18]

As it turned out, apparently neither Ford nor anyone else
would fund the project.

The outcome of this project, along with other failures
to see key ideas propagated through the medium of film,
which Huxley realized could reach far more people than the
written word, must have been disappointing to him.   In
these later years it was not only the financial rewards which
prompted Huxley's interest in film, but his desire to use film
as a medium for education.   This is not to say that he would
not take on film projects to supplement his income; for example, there was the somewhat bizarre work for UPA studios,
as he reported in February 1957, writing an outline "for an
animated cartoon of Don Quixote, to be played by the engaging UPA character, Mr. Magoo."[19] But primarily, he had
come to see film as a way of reaching wider audiences, in
his quest to make people more aware and to encourage their
greatest potentialities.

These last years in Huxley's life brought some tragic
personal events which would affect his professional life as
well as test his own spiritual resilience.   In February 1955
his wife Maria died of cancer.   This was a difficult year for
Huxley, although he busied himself with his play and novel,
The Genius and the Goddess.   A little more than a year later
he married Laura Archera, an Italian twenty years his junior.
She had been a concert violinist, had worked as a film cutter
with Gabriel Pascal, and was currently involved in psycho-
therapy--which was compatible with Huxley's interest in both
psychology and parapsychology.   They moved to a house in
the Hollywood hills at 3276 Deronda Drive; sadly, this house
would be destroyed by a brush fire sweeping the area in
May 1961.   Huxley lost everything--his letters, journals,
books, manuscripts--except the manuscript of the novel he
was working on, Island.   The loss of this collection, including many year's worth of correspondence with some of the
world's most notable figures, obviously was a great blow.
And yet, leave it to Huxley to remark to Anita Loos about
the fire that "It was quite an experience, but it does make
one feel extraordinarily clean."[20] The Huxleys gradually put
their lives back together, moving nearby to 6233 Mulholland
Highway.   As debilitating as these events had been, Huxley
remained remarkably self-possessed, perhaps due to his own
spiritual enlightenment.

As we know, it was enlightenment, and awareness,
which Huxley wished to stimulate in his readers and film-goers.
Whether through feature films, documentaries, or adaptations

of his own books and stories--as well as through writing and
lecturing--Huxley was concerned to save man from himself.
Even in 1963, the last year of his life, he was thinking of
film projects. In March there was the possibility of doing a
screenplay for his friend George Cukor based on Trevor
Hall's 1962 book, The Spiritualists: The Story of Florence
Cook and William Crookes. In November he was talking about
an adaptation for television of his short story (from his 1922
collection Mortal Coils), "The Tillotson Banquet," a psychological study of a painter--just a few days before his death
at age sixty-nine from cancer, on November 22 (a date he
shares with Kennedy's assassination).[21] Huxley asked Laura
towards the end to give him an injection of LSD; intense
awareness at the ultimate moment.[22]

Huxley had chosen as his motto "Aún aprendo"--"I am
still learning." It was with this spirit that he approached
everything, in his personal as well as his professional life.
In his career as a writer he produced many works dealing with
ideas of long-lasting significance and influence. In his career
as a screenwriter, though he faced some disappointments in
seeing his projects produced (his recoil as a writer at the
need for collaboration thus justified), his work which did
reach the screen was, as we have seen, of very fine quality
indeed.

What is important is that Huxley had realized and worked
with the power of cinema--a power to disseminate ideas and
influence people's behavior, as well as to entertain. In a
1963 taped interview Huxley reaffirmed what he had been
striving for in his work for years--to provoke awareness in
people, which would lead them to actualize their "desirable
potentialities": "intelligence, friendliness, creativity." And
he said that social awareness, of such things as the problems
caused by technology and overpopulation, begins with indi-
vidual awareness--by better training in methods of perception,
in the "non-verbal humanities."[23] To this end, Huxley's last
work, Island, with its myna bird shouting "Attention. Attention," showed us an antidote to the evils of Brave New World.
And also to that end, Huxley's intentions were to make us see
more--with the mind's eye.

NOTES

Chapter I: Background

First Impressions

1. Letter 84, to his father Leonard Huxley, March 19, 1916, in Grover Smith, ed., Letters of Aldous Huxley (New York and Evanston: Harper & Row, Publishers, 1969), pp. 94-95.

2. Letter 140, to his brother Julian Huxley, July 21, 1918, in Smith, pp. 157-158.

3. Arnold Hauser, The Social History of Art, Vol. II (New York: Alfred A. Knopf, 1951), p. 940.

4. Rachel Low, The History of the British Film: 1918-1929 (London: George Allen & Unwin Ltd., 1971), p. 305.

5. Craig, quoted in The Bioscope, February 9, 1922, p. 7; cited in Low, p. 18. Drinkwater, quoted in The Bioscope, April 3, 1923, p. 13; cited in Low, p. 18.

6. Other films by Julian Huxley include those made in conjunction with the Eugenics Society and Gaumont-British Films: Heredity in Man, Heredity in Animals, and From Generation to Generation. For more on Julian's work, see Rachel Low's two volumes in The History of the British Film, 1929-1939: Films of Comment and Persuasion of the 1930s, and Documentary and Educational Films of the 1930s (London: George Allen & Unwin, 1979).

7. The following guide reprints the film programs in their entirety: The Film Society Programmes, 1925-1939, prepared under the direction of the Council of the London Film Society (New York: Arno Press, 1972).

8. François Truffaut, Hitchcock, trans. Helen G. Scott (New York: Simon and Schuster, 1967), p. 89.

Fear and Loathing of Mass Culture

9. Aldous Huxley, Antic Hay and The Gioconda Smile (New York: Harper & Brothers, Publishers, 1957), p. 29.

10. Aldous Huxley, Those Barren Leaves (New York: Harper & Brothers, Publishers, 1925), p. 117.

11. Aldous Huxley, Jesting Pilate: The Diary of a Journey (1926; rpt. London: Chatto & Windus, 1948), p. 267.

12. Wodehouse, cited in David A. Jasen, P. G. Wodehouse: A Portrait of a Master (New York: Mason & Lipscomb Publishers, 1974), p. 125.

13. Hortense Powdermaker, Hollywood: The Dream Factory (London: Secker & Warburg, 1951), p. 39.

14. Jesting Pilate, p. 276.

15. Aldous Huxley, "The Outlook for American Culture: Some Reflections in a Machine Age," Harper's Magazine, August 1927, p. 265. Hereafter cited as "Outlook."

16. "Outlook," p. 268.

17. "Outlook," p. 268.

18. Cited in Low, The History of the British Film: 1918-1929, p. 211.

19. Jesting Pilate, p. 287.

20. Aldous Huxley, "Silence Is Golden," in Do What You Will (1929; rpt. London: Chatto & Windus, 1949), p. 54.

21. "Silence Is Golden," pp. 60-61.

22. Aldous Huxley, Brave New World (New York: Harper & Row, Publishers, 1932; Perennial Library, 1969), p. 36.

23. *Brave New World*, p. 86.

24. *Brave New World*, p. 112.

25. On musical shows in cinemas, and on cinema organs, see Low, *The History of the British Film: 1918-1929*, pp. 38-39, and pp. 201-202.

26. *Brave New World*, p. 113.

27. Paul Fussell, *Abroad: British Literary Traveling Between the Wars* (New York: Oxford University Press, 1980), p. 123. Also see Anne Chisholm, *Nancy Cunard: A Biography* (New York: Alfred A. Knopf, 1979).

28. Aldous Huxley, *Eyeless in Gaza* (New York: Harper & Row, Publishers, 1936; Perennial Library, 1974), p. 310. Future references are cited in the body of the text.

29. Fussell, p. 36.

30. Joseph Frank, "Spatial Form in Modern Literature" (1945), in *The Widening Gyre: Crisis and Mastery in Modern Literature* (New Brunswick, N.J.: Rutgers University Press, 1963), p. 59.

31. Robert Phillip Kolker, *A Cinema of Loneliness: Penn, Kubrick, Coppola, Scorsese, Altman* (New York: Oxford University Press, 1980), p. 12.

The Artist Against the Collective

32. Letter 458, to Miss Hepworth and Mr. Green, 1942, in Smith, p. 474.

33. Letter 243, February 3, 1926, in Smith, p. 266.

34. Anonymous reviewer in London, *New York Times*, April 27, 1931, p. 24.

35. Letter 303, February 17, 1930, in Smith, p. 329.

36. Letter 302, February 11, 1930, in Smith, p. 328.

37. Hauser, p. 947.

From Limbo to Los Angeles

38. Fussell, p. 11.

39. On these German and English emigrés to Los An-
geles, see John Baxter, The Hollywood Exiles (New York:
Taplinger Publishing Co., 1976); also useful is Salka Viertel,
The Kindness of Strangers (New York: Holt, Rinehart and
Winston, 1969).   The German expatriate writers (such as
Viertel, Thomas Mann, and Bertolt Brecht) who congregated
in Hollywood have recently been the subject of a play by
Christopher Hampton entitled Tales From Hollywood, which
received its premiere at the Mark Taper Forum in Los An-
geles in March 1982.

40. See Hermann Kesten, ed., Thomas Mann: Diaries
1918-1939, trans. by Richard and Clara Winston (New York:
Harry N. Abrams, Inc., Publishers, 1982), p. 275.   The
Manns and the Huxleys also saw each other in Los Angeles.
Mann's diary entry for April 14, 1938 reports an incident
which Huxley would later use as the basis for an essay on
a sewage-polluted Los Angeles beach, "Hyperion to a Satyr,"
in Adonis and the Alphabet (1956):   "Outing to the beach with
the Huxleys, the weather clearing rapidly and becoming warmer,
where we got out and took a rather long walk along the glis-
tening blue-and-white ocean at ebb tide.   Many condoms on
the beach.   I did not see them, but Mrs. Huxley pointed them
out to Katia" (p. 297).

41. Maria to Roy Fenton, according to Smith's footnote
to Letter 403, Huxley to Eugene F. Saxton, December 24,
1936, in Smith, p. 410.

42. Letter 412, to Julian Huxley, in Smith, p. 421.

43. Letter 413, to Julian Huxley, in Smith, p. 422.

44. Letter 415, to Jacob Zeitlin, July 12, 1937, in
Smith, p. 424.

45. Maria to Edward Sackville-West, from San Cristobal, New Mexico, probably written in late August 1937, cited
in Sybille Bedford, Aldous Huxley: A Biography (New York:
Alfred A. Knopf/Harper & Row, 1973, 1974), p. 358.

46. Peter Firchow, Aldous Huxley: Satirist and Novelist (Minneapolis: University of Minnesota Press, 1972), footnote, p. 159. According to Firchow, the Success manuscript
is in the Manuscript Collection of Stanford University Library
(footnote, p. 171).

47. Brave New World, p. 119.

48. Letter 418, to Julian Huxley, December 6, 1937,
in Smith, p. 428.

49. Letter 417, to Roy Fenton, October 13, 1937, in
Smith, pp. 425-426.

50. Aldous Huxley, After Many a Summer Dies the
Swan (New York: Harper & Row, Publishers, 1939; A Perennial Classic, 1965), p. 9.

51. After Many a Summer, p. 9.

52. Letter 417, in Smith, p. 426.

53. Letter 417, in Smith, pp. 426-427. Sybille Bedford reports that she thinks the "nice mad-man" Maria refers
to was John Davenport; see Bedford, p. 350.

54. Reported by an unnamed friend of Huxley, cited
in Christopher Rand, Los Angeles: The Ultimate City (New
York: Oxford University Press, 1967), p. 195.

55. The quotations are from the following:
        Walpole, cited in Rupert Hart-Davis, Hugh Walpole:
A Biography (New York: Harcourt, Brace & World, Inc.,
1952), pp. 360-361;
        J. B. Priestley, Margin Released: A Writer's Rem-
iniscences and Reflections (New York and Evanston: Harper
& Row, Publishers, 1962), p. 216;
        Coward, cited in Cole Lesley, Remembered Laughter:
The Life of Noel Coward (New York: Alfred A. Knopf, 1976),
p. 142;
        Anthony Powell, Faces in My Time, Vol. III of To
Keep the Ball Rolling (New York: Holt, Rinehart and Winston,
1980), p. 73;
        Maugham, cited in Frederick Raphael, W. Somerset

Maugham and His World (New York: Charles Scribner's Sons,
1976), p. 89.

56.   P. G. Wodehouse, America, I Like You (New York:
Simon and Schuster, 1956), p. 175.

57.   See Powell's reminiscences of Huxley in Lawrence
Clark Powell, California Classics: The Creative Literature of
the Golden State (Los Angeles: The Ward Ritchie Press, 1971),
pp. 357-370.

58.   George Woodcock, Dawn and the Darkest Hour: A
Study of Aldous Huxley (New York: The Viking Press, 1972),
p. 217.

59.   Letter 418, to Julian Huxley, December 6, 1937,
in Smith, p. 428.

60.   Maria to Charles de Noailles, December 30, 1937,
cited in Bedford, p. 364.

61.   Cited in Bedford, p. 371.

62.   Letter 247, to Anita Loos, in Smith, pp. 269-270.

63.   Letter 250, to Julian Huxley, August 10, 1926, in
Smith, p. 272.

Chapter II: Films

The Romance of Science: "Madame Curie"

1.   I have examined Salka Viertel's outline for Madame
Curie, dated 6-4-38 and 6-7-38, in the vault at M-G-M.
        Also see Salka Viertel, The Kindness of Strangers
(New York: Holt, Rinehart and Winston, 1969), pp. 217-239,
where she describes her role in initiating the project at M-G-M;
her meeting with Huxley; and how she researched the project
in Paris in 1939, after Huxley and Fitzgerald had each made attempts at the treatment, only for her to return to California
and learn that the project had been shelved for the time being.

2.   Cited in Sybille Bedford, Aldous Huxley: A Biography (New York: Alfred A. Knopf/Harper & Row, 1973,
1974), p. 360.

3.   Letter 425, to Julian Huxley, in Grover Smith, ed., Letters of Aldous Huxley (New York and Evanston: Harper & Row, Publishers, 1969), p. 436.

4.   Letter 427, in Smith, p. 437.

5.   Aldous Huxley, Crome Yellow (New York: Harper & Row, Publishers, 1922), p. 215 and p. 217.

6.   Letter 427, in Smith, p. 437.

7.   Raymond Chandler, "Writers in Hollywood," in Highlights From 125 Years of the Atlantic, ed. by Louise Desaulniers (Boston: The Atlantic Monthly Company, 1977), p. 408.

8.   Letter 427, in Smith, p. 437.

9.   Aaron Latham, Crazy Sundays: F. Scott Fitzgerald in Hollywood (New York: The Viking Press, 1971), p. 196.

10.   Letter to Messrs. Berg, Dozier and Allen, in Correspondence of F. Scott Fitzgerald, ed. by Matthew J. Bruccoli and Margaret M. Duggan (New York: Random House, 1980), p. 582.

11.   Bosley Crowther, "Afterthoughts on Madame Curie and Two Other Films," New York Times, January 9, 1944, section II, p. 3.   Crowther's first review of the film was on December 17, 1943, p. 23.

12.   Anita Loos, Kiss Hollywood Goodbye (New York: The Viking Press, 1974), p. 155.

13.   Robert Reid, Marie Curie (New York: Saturday Review Press/E. P. Dutton & Co., Inc., 1974), cited on p. 196.

14.   Aldous Huxley, The Genius and the Goddess (New York: Harper & Brothers, 1955), p. 99 and p. 154.

15.   Eve Curie, Madame Curie: A Biography, trans. by Vincent Sheean (1937; rpt. New York: Garden City Publishing Co., Inc., 1940), p. 225.

16.   The Genius and the Goddess, p. 119.

17.   Letter 780, November 21, 1957, in Smith, pp. 831-832.

Shall We Dance?:   "Pride and Prejudice"

18.   Anita Loos, in Aldous Huxley, 1894-1963:   A Memorial Volume, ed. by Julian Huxley (New York: Harper & Row, Publishers, 1965), p. 95.

19.   Letter 436, Huxley to his American publisher Eugene Saxton, in Smith, p. 447.

20.   Polonsky, quoted in Hollywood Voices: Interviews with Film Directors, ed. by Andrew Sarris (Indianapolis and New York: The Bobbs-Merrill Company, Inc., 1967, 1971), pp. 142-143.

21.   Letter 436, in Smith, p. 447.

22.   George Bluestone, Novels into Film (Baltimore: The Johns Hopkins Press, 1957), p. 118.

23.   Jane Austen, Pride and Prejudice (1813; rpt. New York: The New American Library, Inc., 1961), p. 5.   Future chapter and page references are to this edition, and are cited in the body of the text.

24.   Helen Jerome, "Pride and Prejudice," in The Best Plays of 1935-36, ed. by Burns Mantle (New York: Dodd, Mead and Company, 1966), pp. 357-361.

25.   Copies of Zoë Akins' 116-page script are at both the UCLA Theatre Arts Library, and The American Film Institute's Louis B. Mayer Library in Los Angeles.

26.   Copies of Huxley-Murfin's 162-page script are at both the UCLA Theatre Arts Library and The American Film Institute's Louis B. Mayer Library in Los Angeles.   Future references will be to this script, or are a transcription directly from the film.   I have also used the "Dialogue Cutting Continuity" of Pride and Prejudice by film editor Robert J. Kern, dated July 1, 1940, at the Motion Picture Division of the Library of Congress.

27. David Daiches, "Jane Austen, Karl Marx and the Aristocratic Dance," American Scholar, XVII (Summer, 1948), p. 291, cited in Bluestone, p. 127.

28. Bluestone, p. 131.

29. Maria to her sister Jeanne, 1940, cited in Bedford, p. 390.

Love Among the Ruins: "Jane Eyre"

30. Information on Ketti Frings' contribution is from the "Data for Bulletin of Screen Achievement Records"; this is on file, along with the studio publicity release regarding Welles' contribution to Jane Eyre, at the Margaret Herrick Library of the Academy of Motion Picture Arts and Sciences, in Beverly Hills.

31. For the story of these negotiations, see Letter 445 (August 14, 1940) and Letter 446 (October 6, 1940), from Huxley to Frieda Lawrence, in Smith, pp. 455-459. The film of Lawrence's work was eventually made as L'Amant de Lady Chatterley (Marc Allégret, 1959); and a British version, Lady Chaterley's Lover (Just Jaeckin, 1981).

32. According to William Torbert Leonard, Theatre: Stage to Screen to Television, Vol. I (Metuchen, N.J. and London: The Scarecrow Press, Inc., 1981), p. 771. Other credits include: director, John Larkin; screenplay, Tom Bridges and George Root, Jr.; Charlotte Brontë played by Molly Lamont; Emily Brontë played by Lynne Roberts.

33. Cited in Bedford, p. 415.

34. Letter 456, to Mrs. Flora Strousse, November 17, 1941, in Smith, p. 471.

35. Interview between Christopher Isherwood and Fred Lawrence Guiles, November 3, 1973, in Guiles, Hanging On in Paradise (New York: McGraw-Hill, 1975), cited on p. 32. Isherwood's screen credits include Little Friend 1934, Rage in Heaven 1941, Forever and a Day 1944, Adventure in Baltimore 1949, The Great Sinner 1949, Diane 1956, The Loved One 1965, The Sailor from Gibralter 1968, and Frankenstein, the

True Story 1973. On Isherwood's film work and life in California, see Isherwood, My Guru and His Disciple (New York:
Farrar, Straus, Giroux, 1980); and Gilbert Adair, "Isherwood
in Hollywood," Sight and Sound, 46 (Winter 1976), p. 25.

36. Curiously, this 154-page script, whose cover is
stamped with the war-time slogan "Less Shooting Here Means
More Shooting Over There--Save Film!", lists no authors.
Copies of the script are at the UCLA Theatre Arts Library,
and The American Film Institute's Louis B. Mayer Library in
Los Angeles. There is also a dialogue continuity, marked
"Dialogue Taken From the Screen. Sept. 15, 1943" at the
Motion Picture Division of the Library of Congress. Future
references are either to this shooting script or to this dia-
logue continuity.

37. Michael Riley, "Gothic Melodrama and Spiritual Romance: Vision and Fidelity in Two Versions of Jane Eyre,"
Literature/Film Quarterly, Vol. III, No. 2, Spring 1975, p.
148.

38. Riley, p. 151.

39. Charlotte Brontë, Jane Eyre (1847; rpt. New York:
Random House, 1943), Ch. 15, p. 107. Future references
are to this edition and are made in the body of the text.

40. Letter 604, to Grover Smith, March 3, 1952, in
Smith, p. 640.

41. Motion Picture Herald, January 29, 1944, p. 32.

42. Orson Welles, cited in Louis Giannetti, Masters of
the American Cinema (Englewood Cliffs, N.J.: Prentice-Hall,
Inc., 1981), p. 275.

Between Takes

43. Letter 486, to Mrs. Grace Hubble, May 10, 1944,
in Smith, p. 505.

44. Letter 484, April 10, 1944, in Smith, p. 502.

45. Letter 491, in Smith, p. 510.

46. Letter 490, July 22, 1944, in Smith, p. 509 and p. 510.

47. Letter 508, October 13, 1945, in Smith, p. 535.

48. Aldous Huxley, Crome Yellow (New York: Harper & Row, Publishers, 1922), p. 289 and p. 40.

49. Letter 509, to Victoria Ocampo, November 24, 1945, in Smith, p. 537.

50. Letter 508, October 13, 1945, in Smith, p. 534.

51. Letter 508, in Smith, p. 535.

52. See Huxley's letters to Loos: Letter 536, March 9, 1947, in Smith, pp. 567-568; and Letter 537, March 26, 1947, in Smith, p. 569.

53. Letter 509, November 24, 1945, in Smith, p. 537.

54. See Letter 511, Huxley to Julian Huxley, March 18, 1946, in Smith, p. 539; and Letter 753, Huxley to Dr. Humphrey Osmond, August 13, 1956, in Smith, p. 805.

55. Letter 757, Huxley to Matthew and Ellen Huxley, September 30, 1956, in Smith, p. 808. Franklin Lacey's involvement with the Brave New World musical project is as according to a telephone interview with Mrs. Franklin Lacey, Los Angeles, April 24, 1986.

56. Letter 757, in Smith, p. 809.

57. On negotiations regarding Brave New World: See Letter 770, Huxley to Robert Craft, re Stravinsky, March 26, 1957, in Smith, pp. 820-821; and Letter 771, Huxley to Leonard Bernstein, April 4, 1957, in Smith, p. 821. See Letter 769, Huxley to Matthew and Ellen Huxley, March 24, 1957, in Smith, p. 820. See Letter 934, Huxley to Daniel O'Shea (representing RKO), September 5, 1963, in Smith, pp. 957-958.

Alone At Last: "A Woman's Vengeance"

58. Aldous Huxley, "The Gioconda Smile," Collected

Short Stories (1957; rpt. London: Chatto & Windus, 1969),
p. 106 and p. 117.

    59. Letter 522, October 4, 1946, in Smith, pp. 549-
550.

    60. Letter 541, to Anita Loos, July 4, 1947, in Smith,
p. 572.

    61. Letter 540, to Matthew Huxley, June 17, 1947, in
Smith, p. 571.

    62. Letter 541, in Smith, p. 572.

    63. Letter 541, in Smith, p. 572.

    64. Aldous Huxley, Ape and Essence (New York:
Harper & Row, Publishers, 1948; A Perennial Classic, 1972),
p. 4.

    65. Letter 545, to Gervas Huxley, November 14, 1947,
in Smith, p. 576.

    66. Letter 535, February 14, 1947, in Smith, p. 566.

    67. Letter 535, in Smith, p. 566.

    68. See Letter 529, to John Van Druten, December 14,
1946, and Smith's footnote to it, in Smith, p. 560. Also see
Aldous Huxley, The Gioconda Smile: A Play in Three Acts,
From the Short Story (London: Samuel French, 1948).

    69. François Truffaut, Hitchcock, trans. by Helen G.
Scott (New York: Simon & Schuster, 1967), p. 12.

    70. I was not able to examine the shooting script of
A Woman's Vengeance. Quotations from the film are based on
my transcription of the film, viewed at the Library of Congress.

    71. Hitchcock, cited in Truffaut, p. 50.

    72. W. A. Darlington, review of the London production
of The Gioconda Smile, New York Times, June 20, 1948, section
II, p. 2.

73. André Bazin, What Is Cinema?, Vol. I, ed. and trans. by Hugh Gray (Berkeley and Los Angeles: University of California Press, 1967), p. 86.

74. Hitchcock, cited in Truffaut, p. 50.

75. Letter 535, in Smith, p. 566.

Chapter III: "California" Novels

The Writer in Hollywood

1. Nathanael West, in a letter to a friend while on his way back to Hollywood from New York, 1938, cited in Tom Dardis, Some Time in the Sun (New York: Charles Scribner's Sons, 1976), p. 156.

2. Jonas Spatz, Hollywood in Fiction: Some Versions of the American Myth (The Hague and Paris: Mouton & Co., 1969), pp. 9-10.

For other studies of the writers and fiction of Hollywood, see the bibliography.

California Dreaming: "After Many a Summer Dies the Swan"

3. Guest list is as according to Sybille Bedford, Aldous Huxley: A Biography (New York: Alfred A. Knopf/Harper & Row, 1973, 1974), p. 381.

4. Information on the writing of Citizen Kane can be found in Pauline Kael, The Citizen Kane Book (Boston: Atlantic Monthly/Little Brown, 1971), which also includes both the shooting script and the cutting continuity; useful, although Kael's bias towards Mankiewicz as author seems groundless. Kael does not mention Huxley's After Many a Summer Dies the Swan.

5. Maria to Edward Sackville-West, October 14, 1938, cited in Bedford, p. 376.

6. Letter 429, to Harold Raymond, February 19, 1939, in Grover Smith, ed., Letters of Aldous Huxley (New York and Evanston: Harper & Row, Publishers, 1969), p. 440.

7. W. H. Auden, "Psychology and Art To-day," in The Arts To-day, ed. by Geoffrey Grigson (London: John Lane The Bodley Head, 1935), p. 20; cited in Samuel Hynes, The Auden Generation: Literature and Politics in England in the 1930s (New York: The Viking Press, 1977), p. 14.

8. Hynes, p. 15.

9. Letter 431, to Julian Huxley, July 30, 1939, in Smith, p. 441.

10. On Menippean satire, see Northrop Frye, Anatomy of Criticism: Four Essays (Princeton: Princeton University Press, 1957), pp. 308-312. I have also made use of Frye's discussion of satire and its stages in the section "The Mythos of Winter: Irony and Satire," pp. 223-239.

11. Aldous Huxley, After Many a Summer Dies the Swan (New York: Harper & Row, Publishers, 1939; A Perennial Classic, 1965), p. 175. Future references are to this edition and are made in the body of the text.

12. Charles M. Holmes, Aldous Huxley and the Way to Reality (Westport, Conn.: Greenwood Press, Publishers, 1970), p. 126.

13. Peter Bowering, Aldous Huxley: A Study of the Major Novels (London: The Athlone Press of the University of London, 1968), p. 214.

14. Christopher Isherwood, "Los Angeles" (1947), in Exhumations: Stories, Articles, Verse (New York: Simon and Schuster, 1966), p. 161. Another essay useful for its impressions of Santa Monica in particular is "The Shore" (1952), also in this collection.

15. Keith M. May, Aldous Huxley (London: Paul Elek Books Limited, 1972), p. 143.

16. See Letter 435, Huxley to Harold Raymond (his publisher), August 20, 1939, in Smith, p. 446. Huxley also reports here that he has been helped in "the finer shades of the American language" by his friend Anita Loos.

17. Cited in Bedford, p. 379.

18. Aldous Huxley, Eyeless in Gaza (New York: Harper & Row, Publishers, 1936; Perennial Library, 1974), p. 280 (Ch. 31, "Sept. 6, 1933").

19. May, p. 155.

20. Letter 432, to Kingsley Martin, July 30, 1939, in Smith, p. 444.

The Lost Screenplay: "Ape and Essence"

21. Letter to Matthew Huxley, February 22, 1948, cited in Bedford, p. 473.

22. Letter 568, June 9, 1949, in Smith, p. 600.

23. Review by MacCarthy, Sunday Times, February 20, 1949, p. 3, cited in Donald Watt, ed., Aldous Huxley: The Critical Heritage (London and Boston: Routledge & Kegan Paul, 1975), p. 26.

24. Peter Firchow, Aldous Huxley: Satirist and Novelist (Minneapolis: University of Minnesota Press, 1972), p. 134.

25. See Northrop Frye, Anatomy of Criticism: Four Essays (Princeton: Princeton University Press, 1957), pp. 223-239.

26. Aldous Huxley, Ape and Essence (New York: Harper & Row, Publishers, 1948; A Perennial Classic, 1972), p. 1. Future references are to this edition and are made in the body of the text.

27. See Letter 521, to Cass Canfield, September 14, 1946, in Smith, p. 548, and Letter 531, to Mrs. Hannah Closs, January 7, 1947, in Smith, pp. 561-562.

28. George Woodcock, Dawn and the Darkest Hour: A Study of Aldous Huxley (New York: The Viking Press, 1972), p. 256.

29. Aldous Huxley, Brave New World (New York: Harper & Row, Publishers, 1932; Perennial Library, 1969), p. 10.

30. Letter 537, March 26, 1947, in Smith, p. 569.

31. According to Maria Huxley, who said that Aldous
and Matthew Huxley "went to see a Chaplin and a film by
H. G. Wells," cited in Bedford, p. 316. This film had to be
the British film Things to Come (director, William Cameron
Menzies, 1936). The similarity between the scene in Things
to Come about planes, and the scene in Ape and Essence
about trains, has also been noted by Tom Dardis in Some
Time in the Sun (New York: Charles Scribner's Sons, 1976),
p. 167. The lines I quote from Things to Come are based on
my transcription from a viewing of that film.

32. Aldous Huxley, Time Must Have a Stop (New York
and London: Harper & Brothers Publishers, 1944), p. 298.

Conclusion: Slow Fade-Out

1. According to Louis Giannetti, Masters of the American Cinema (Englewood Cliffs, N.J.: Prentice-Hall, Inc.,
1981), p. 20.

2. Letter to Matthew Huxley, December 1947, cited in
Bedford, p. 471. For more on Chaplin and his difficulties,
see "Charlie Chaplin's Monsieur Verdoux Press Conference"
(April 12, 1947), Film Comment, Winter, 1969, pp. 34-43; and
Terry Hickey, "Accusations Against Charles Chaplin for Political and Moral Offenses," Film Comment, Winter, 1969, pp.
44-57.

3. Evelyn Waugh, diary entry for April 7, 1947, in
The Diaries of Evelyn Waugh, ed. by Michael Davie (Boston:
Little, Brown and Company, 1976), p. 675.

4. In the Daily Telegraph and Morning Post, April 30,
1947, p. 4, and May 1, 1947, p. 4; reprinted in Evelyn Waugh,
A Little Order: A Selection from His Journalism, ed. by
Donat Gallagher (Boston: Little, Brown and Company, 1977),
p. 36. For more on Waugh's experiences in Hollywood, see
also:
      Christopher Sykes, Evelyn Waugh: A Biography (Bos-
ton: Little, Brown and Company, 1975), pp. 300-312;
      Mark Amory, ed., The Letters of Evelyn Waugh (New
Haven and New York: Ticknor & Fields, 1980), pp. 247-266.

Malcolm Bradbury, "America and the Comic Vision," in Evelyn Waugh and His World, ed. by David Pryce-Jones (Boston: Little, Brown and Company, 1973), pp. 166-182. A useful essay on The Loved One and other "California" novels.

5. Letter from Maria, April 1948, cited in Bedford, p. 478.

6. See, for example, Letter 552, Huxley to Julian Huxley, June 3, 1948, in Smith, p. 582.

7. Letter 561, to Matthew Huxley, March 6, 1949, in Smith, p. 593.

8. Igor Stravinsky and Robert Craft, Dialogues and a Diary (London: Faber and Faber, 1968), p. 94. The book is also useful for impressions of Evelyn Waugh, Gerald Heard, Christopher Isherwood, as well as of Huxley. See pp. 91-179.

9. Stravinsky and Craft, p. 156.

10. Letter from Maria, 1951, cited in Bedford, p. 502.

11. Aldous Huxley, Ape and Essence (New York: Harper & Row, Publishers, 1948; A Perennial Classic, 1972), p. 1. Subsequent references are made in the body of the text.

12. Letter 608, Huxley to Julian Huxley, May 20, 1952, in Smith, pp. 644-645.

13. Letter 618, Huxley to Julian Huxley, January 25, 1953, in Smith, p. 663.

14. Frank Capra, The Name Above the Title: An Autobiography (New York: The Macmillan Co., 1971), p. 441.

15. Aldous Huxley, The Doors of Perception and Heaven and Hell (New York: Harper & Row Publishers, 1956), p. 169.

16. Letter 674, Huxley to Matthew and Ellen Huxley, in Smith, p. 716.

17. Heaven and Hell, p. 168.

18. Letter 772, Huxley to Dr. Humphrey Osmond,
April 8, 1957, in Smith, p. 822.

19. Letter 768, Huxley to Dr. Humphrey Osmond,
February 22, 1957, in Smith, p. 819.

20. In a telephone call Anita Loos made to Huxley, according to Sybille Bedford; see Sybille Bedford, Aldous Huxley: A Biography (New York: Alfred A. Knopf/Harper &
Row, 1973, 1974), p. 659. The fire occurred on May 12, 1961.

21. Letter 923, Huxley to Mrs. Eileen J. Garrett of
the Parapsychology Foundation, March 27, 1963, in Smith,
p. 951; and Letter 943, Huxley to Max Kester (dictated, text
from Laura Huxley's transcription of the sound tape), November 17, in Smith, p. 964.

22. For an account of Huxley's later years, see Laura
Archera Huxley, This Timeless Moment: A Personal View of
Aldous Huxley (New York: Farrar, Straus & Giroux, 1968).

23. A Conversation with Aldous Huxley, "A 1963 discussion with the renowned novelist and philosopher." #12215
(North Hollywood, CA: The Center for Cassette Studies, Inc.,
1963).

FILMOGRAPHY

MADAME CURIE, Metro-Goldwyn-Mayer, 1943 (Aldous Huxley's treatment of 1938 was uncredited)

screenplay: Paul Osborn and Paul H. Rameau
source material: Madame Curie (1937), a biography by Eve Curie
director: Mervyn LeRoy
producer: Sidney Franklin
narration spoken by: James Hilton
musical score: Herbert Stothart
director of photography: Joseph Ruttenberg
recording director: Douglas Shearer
art director: Cedric Gibbons
   associate: Paul Groesse
set decorations: Edwin B. Willis
   associate: Hugh Hunt
special effects: Warren Newcombe
costume supervision: Irene
   associate: [Irene] Sharaff
men's costumes: Gile Steele
make-up created by: Jack Dawn
film editor: Harold F. Kress

Greer Garson (Mme. Curie)
Walter Pidgeon (Pierre Curie)
Henry Travers (Eugene Curie)
Albert Basserman (Prof. Jean Perot)
Robert Walker (David LeGros)
C. Aubrey Smith (Lord Kelvin)
Dame May Whitty (Mme. Eugene Curie, Sr.)
Victor Francen (President of University)
Elsa Basserman (Mme. Perot)
Reginald Owen (Dr. Becquerel)
Van Johnson (Reporter)
Margaret O'Brien (Irene)

PRIDE AND PREJUDICE, Metro-Goldwyn-Mayer, 1940

screenplay: Aldous Huxley and Jane Murfin
source material: novel by Jane Austen, as dramatized by
    Helen Jerome
director: Robert Z. Leonard
producer: Hunt Stromberg
musical score: Herbert Stothart
director of photography: Karl Freund
recording director: Douglas Shearer
art director: Cedric Gibbons
    associate: Paul Groesse
set decorations: Edwin B. Willis
gowns: Adrian
men's costumes: Gile Steele
hair stylist: Sydney Guilaroff
make-up created by: Jack Dawn
dance direction: Ernst Matray
technical advisor: George Richelavie
film editor: Robert J. Kern

Those Living at Meryton Village:

Edward Ashley (Mr. Wickham)
Marten Lamont (Mr. Denny)
E. E. Clive (Sir William Lucas)
Marjorie Wood (Lady Lucas)
May Beatty (Mrs. Philips)

Those LIving at Longbourn:

Greer Garson (Elizabeth Bennet)
Maureen O'Sullivan (Jane Bennet)
Ann Rutherford (Lydia Bennet)
Marsha Hunt (Mary Bennet)
Heather Angel (Kitty Bennet)
Mary Boland (Mrs. Bennet
Edmund Gwenn (Mr. Bennet)

Those Living at Netherfield:

Laurence Olivier (Mr. Darcy)
Frieda Inescort (Miss Bingley)
Bruce Lester (Mr. Bingley)

Those Living at Rosings:

Edna May Oliver (Lady Catherine de Bourgh)
Gia Kent (Anne de Bourgh)
Melville Cooper (Mr. Collins)
Karen Morley (Mrs. Collins)

JANE EYRE, Twentieth Century-Fox, 1944

screenplay: Aldous Huxley, Robert Stevenson and John
    Houseman
source material: novel by Charlotte Brontë
director: Robert Stevenson
producer: William Goetz
music: Bernard Herrmann
director of photography: George Barnes
production designed by: William Pereira
art direction: James Basevi, Wiard B. Ihnen
set decorations: Thomas Little
    associate: Ross Dowd
costumes: Rene Hubert
scenario assistant: Barbara Keon
make-up artist: Guy Pearce
special photographic effects: Fred Sersen
sound: W. D. Flick, Roger Heman
film editor: Walter Thompson

Orson Welles (Edward Rochester)
Joan Fontaine (Jane Eyre)
Peggy Ann Garner (Jane as a child)
Margaret O'Brien (Adele Varens)
Elizabeth Taylor (Helen Burns)
John Sutton (Dr. John Rivers)
Sara Allgood (Bessie)
Henry Daniell (Mr. Brocklehurst)
Agnes Moorehead (Mrs. Read)
Aubrey Mather (Colonel Dent)
Edith Barrett (Mrs. Fairfax)
Barbara Everest (Lady Ingram)
Hillary Brooke (Blanche Ingram)
Ethel Griffies (Grace Poole)
Mae Marsh (Leah)
Eily Malyon (Miss Scatcherd)
Mary Forbes (Mrs. Eshton)

Thomas London (Sir George Lynn)
Yorke Sherwood (Beadle)
Ivan Simpson (Mr. Wood)
Erskine Sanford (Mr. Briggs)
John Abbott (Mason)
Ronald Harris (John)
Charles Irwin (Auctioneer)

A WOMAN'S VENGEANCE, Universal-International, 1947

screenplay: Aldous Huxley
source material: "The Gioconda Smile" (1922), a story by
    Aldous Huxley
director: Zoltan Korda
producer: Zoltan Korda
music: Miklos Rozsa
director of photography: Russell Metty
art direction: Bernard Herzbrun, Eugene Lourie
assistant to producer: Fred Pressburger
assistant director: Horace Hough
costumes designed by: Orry Kelly
sound: Leslie I. Carey, Corson Jewett
set decorations: Russell A. Gausman, T. F. Offenbecker
hair stylist: Carmen Dirigo
make-up: Bud Westmore
film editor: Jack Wheeler

Charles Boyer (Henry Maurier)
Jessica Tandy (Janet Spence)
Sir Cedric Hardwicke (Dr. Libbard)
Ann Blyth (Doris)
Mildred Natwick (Nurse Braddock)
Cecil Humphreys (General Spence)
Hugh French (Robert Lester)
Rachel Kempson (Emily Maurier)
Valerie Cardew (Clara)
Carl Harbord (Coroner)
John Williams (Prosecuting Counsel)
Leland Hodgson (First Warder)
Ola Lorraine (Maisey)
Harry Cording (McNabb)

SELECTED BIBLIOGRAPHY

WORKS BY HUXLEY (Including Novels in toto; Arranged
Chronologically)

Huxley, Aldous. Crome Yellow. 1921; rpt. New York:
Harper & Row, Publishers, 1922.

_____. "The Gioconda Smile" (1922). Collected Short
Stories. 1957; rpt. London: Chatto & Windus, 1969.

_____. Antic Hay and The Gioconda Smile. 1923; rpt.
New York: Harper & Row, Publishers, 1957.

_____. Those Barren Leaves. New York: Harper & Row,
Publishers, 1925.

_____. Jesting Pilate: The Diary of a Journey. 1926;
rpt. London: Chatto & Windus, 1948.

_____. "The Outlook for American Culture: Some Reflec-
tions in a Machine Age." Harper's Magazine, August,
1927, pp. 265-272.

_____. Point Counter Point. New York: Harper & Row,
Publishers, 1928.

_____. "Silence Is Golden." Do What You Will. 1929; rpt.
London: Chatto & Windus, 1949.

_____. Brave New World. New York: Harper & Row,
Publishers, 1932; Perennial Library, 1969.

_____. Eyeless in Gaza. New York: Harper & Row, Pub-
lishers, 1936; Perennial Library, 1974.

135

_____. After Many a Summer Dies the Swan. New York: Harper & Row, Publishers, 1939; A Perennial Classic, 1965.

_____. Time Must Have a Stop. New York: Harper & Row, Publishers, 1944.

_____. The Gioconda Smile: A Play in Three Acts, From the Short Story. London: Samuel French, 1948.

_____. Ape and Essence. New York: Harper & Row, Publishers, 1948; A Perennial Classic, 1972.

_____. The Genius and the Goddess. New York: Harper & Row, Publishers, 1955.

_____. The Doors of Perception and Heaven and Hell. New York: Harper & Row, Publishers, 1956.

_____. Island. New York: Harper & Row, Publishers, 1962.

WORKS ABOUT HUXLEY

Atkins, John. Aldous Huxley: A Literary Study. New York: The Orion Press, 1967.

Bedford, Sybille. Aldous Huxley: A Biography. New York: Alfred A. Knopf/ Harper & Row, 1973, 1974.

Bowering, Peter. Aldous Huxley: A Study of the Major Novels. London: The Athlone Press of the University of London, 1968.

Brander, Laurence. Aldous Huxley: A Critical Study. Lewisburg, PA: Bucknell University Press, 1970.

By and About Aldous Huxley: A Bibliography of the Aldous Huxley Collection at Milne Library. Geneseo, NY: Milne Library, State University of New York, College of Arts and Sciences, 1973.

Clark, Ronald. The Huxleys. New York and Toronto: McGraw-Hill Book Company, 1968.

A Conversation with Aldous Huxley. "A 1963 discussion with
    the renowned novelist and philosopher." #12215 (North
    Hollywood, CA: The Center for Cassette Studies, Inc.,
    1963.

Firchow, Peter. Aldous Huxley: Satirist and Novelist.
    Minneapolis: University of Minnesota Press, 1972.

Holmes, Charles M. Aldous Huxley and the Way to Reality.
    Westport, CT: Greenwood Press, Publishers, 1970.

Huxley, Julian, ed. Aldous Huxley, 1894-1963: A Memorial
    Volume. New York: Harper & Row, Publishers, 1965.

Huxley, Laura Archera. This Timeless Moment: A Personal
    View of Aldous Huxley. New York: Farrar, Straus &
    Giroux, 1968.

May, Keith M. Aldous Huxley. London: Paul Elek Books
    Limited, 1972.

Smith, Grover, ed. Letters of Aldous Huxley. New York and
    Evanston: Harper & Row, Publishers, 1969.

Watt, Donald, ed. Aldous Huxley: The Critical Heritage.
    London and Boston: Routledge & Kegan Paul, 1975.

Wickes, George, ed. Aldous Huxley at UCLA: A Catalogue
    of the Manuscripts ... with ... Three Unpublished Letters.
    Los Angeles: University of California Library, 1964.

Woodcock, George. Dawn and the Darkest Hour: A Study
    of Aldous Huxley. New York: The Viking Press, 1972.

WORKS ON THEORIES OF LITERATURE AND OF FILM;
ON NOVELS INTO FILM

Bazin, André. What Is Cinema? Vol. I. Edited and trans-
    lated by Hugh Gray. Berkeley and Los Angeles: Univer-
    sity of California Press, 1967.

Bluestone, George. Novels into Film. Baltimore: Johns
    Hopkins Press, 1957.

Chatman, Seymour. Story and Discourse: Narrative Struc-
    ture in Fiction and Film. Ithaca, NY: Cornell University
    Press, 1978.

Cohen, Keith. Film and Fiction: The Dynamics of Exchange.
    New Haven and London: Yale University Press, 1979.

Ellis, Kate and Kaplan, E. Ann. "Feminism in Brontë's
    Novel and Its Film Versions." The English Novel and the
    Movies. Edited by Michael Klein and Gillian Parker. New
    York: Frederick Ungar Publishing Co., 1981.

Frank, Joseph. "Spatial Form in Modern Literature" (1945).
    The Widening Gyre: Crisis and Mastery in Modern Litera-
    ture. New Brunswick, NJ: Rutgers University Press,
    1963.

Frye, Northrop. Anatomy of Criticism: Four Essays. Prince-
    ton, NJ: Princeton University Press, 1957.

Fussell, Paul. Abroad: British Literary Traveling Between
    the Wars. New York: Oxford University Press, 1980.

Hauser, Arnold. The Social History of Art. Vol II. New
    York: Alfred A. Knopf, 1951.

Hynes, Samuel. The Auden Generation: Literature and Pol-
    itics in England in the 1930s. New York: The Viking
    Press, 1977.

Lellis, George and Bolton, H. Philip. "Pride but No Preju-
    dice." The English Novel and the Movies. Edited by
    Michael Klein and Gillian Parker. New York: Frederick
    Ungar Publishing Co., 1981.

Murray, Edward. The Cinematic Imagination: Writers and the
    Motion Pictures. New York: Frederick Ungar Publishing
    Co., 1972.

Richardson, Robert. Literature and Film. Bloomington and
    London: Indiana University Press, 1969.

Riley, Michael. "Gothic Melodrama and Spiritual Romance:
    Vision and Fidelity in Two Versions of Jane Eyre." Litera-
    ture/Film Quarterly, III, No. 2 (Spring, 1975), 145-159.

Spiegel, Alan. Fiction and the Camera Eye: Visual Consciousness in Film and the Modern Novel. Charlottesville, VA:
University Press of Virginia, 1976.

Wagner, Geoffrey. "Jane Eyre." The Novel and the Cinema.
Cranbury, NJ: Associated University Presses, Inc., 1975.

Wright, Andrew. "Jane Austen Adapted." Nineteenth Century Fiction, Vol. 30, No. 3 (Dec., 1975), 421-453.

GENERAL WORKS ABOUT WRITERS, FILM, AND HOLLYWOOD

Armes, Roy. A Critical History of the British Cinema. New
York: Oxford University Press, 1978.

Baxter, John. The Hollywood Exiles. New York: Taplinger
Publishing Co., 1976.

Brownlow, Kevin. The Parade's Gone By. New York: Alfred A. Knopf, 1968.

Connolly, Cyril. "Introduction." Horizon, No. 93-94 (October, 1947), 1-11. [Special issue: "Art on the American
Horizon"]

Cook, David A. A History of Narrative Film. New York:
W. W. Norton and Company, 1981.

Dardis, Tom. Some Time in the Sun. New York: Charles
Scribner's Sons, 1976.

Davie, Michael. California, the Vanishing Dream. New York:
Dodd, Mead and Company, 1972.

The Film Society Programmes. Prepared under the direction
of the Council of the London Film Society. New York:
Arno Press, 1972.

Finch, Christopher and Rosenkrantz, Linda. Gone Hollywood:
The Movie Colony in the Golden Age. Garden City, NY:
Doubleday and Co., Inc., 1979.

Geduld, Harry M., ed. Authors on Film. Bloomington and
London: Indiana University Press, 1972.

Giannetti, Louis. Masters of the American Cinema. Englewood
Cliffs, NJ: Prentice-Hall, Inc., 1981.

Guiles, Fred Laurence. Hanging On in Paradise. New York:
McGraw-Hill, 1975.

Kael, Pauline. The Citizen Kane Book. Boston: Atlantic
Monthly/Little, Brown, 1971.

Latham, Aaron. Crazy Sundays: F. Scott Fitzgerald in
Hollywood. New York: The Viking Press, 1971.

Lokke, Virgil L. "The Literary Image of Hollywood." Unpublished Ph.D. dissertation, State University of Iowa,
1955.

Loos, Anita. Cast of Thousands. New York: Grosset and
Dunlap, 1977.

_____. Kiss Hollywood Goodbye. New York: The Viking
Press, 1974.

Low, Rachel. The History of the British Film: 1918-1929.
London: George Allen & Unwin Ltd., 1971.

_____. The History of the British Film, 1929-1939: Docu-
mentary and Educational Films of the 1930s. London:
George Allen & Unwin, 1979.

_____. The History of the British Film, 1929-1939: Films
of Comment and Persuasion of the 1930s. London: George
Allen & Unwin, 1979.

McWilliams, Carey. Southern California Country: An Island
on the Land. New York: Duell, Sloan & Pearce, 1946.

Morley, Sheridan. Tales of the Hollywood Raj: The British,
the Movies, and Tinseltown. New York: Viking, 1984.

Powdermaker, Hortense. Hollywood: The Dream Factory.
London: Secker & Warburg, 1951.

Powell, Lawrence Clark. Books West Southwest. Los Angeles:
The Ward Ritchie Press, 1957.

_____. California Classics: The Creative Literature of the Golden State. Los Angeles: The Ward Ritchie Press, 1971.

Rand, Christopher. Los Angeles: The Ultimate City. New York: Oxford University Press, 1967.

Rolfe, Lionel. Literary L.A. San Francisco: Chronicle Books, 1981.

Rosten, Leo. Hollywood: The Movie Colony, the Movie Makers. New York: Harcourt, Brace, 1941.

See, Carolyn. "The Hollywood Novel: An Historical and Critical Study." Unpublished Ph.D. dissertation, U.C.L.A., 1963.

Spatz, Jonas. Hollywood in Fiction: Some Versions of the American Myth. The Hague and Paris: Mouton & Co., 1969.

Stravinsky, Igor and Craft, Robert. Dialogues and a Diary. London: Faber and Faber, 1968.

Taylor, John Russell. Strangers in Paradise: The Hollywood Emigrés, 1933-1950. New York: Holt, Rinehart and Winston, 1983.

Truffaut, François. Hitchcock. Translated by Helen G. Scott. New York: Simon & Schuster, 1967.

Viertel, Salka. The Kindness of Strangers. New York: Holt, Rinehart and Winston, 1969.

Walker, Franklin. A Literary History of Southern California. Berkeley and Los Angeles: University of California Press, 1950.

Wells, Walter. Tycoons and Locusts: A Regional Look at Hollywood Fiction of the 1930s. Carbondale and Edwardsville: Southern Illinois University Press, 1973.

INDEX